D1707541

"New England's Annoyances"

"New England's Annoyances"

America's First Folk Song

J. A. Leo Lemay

Newark: University of Delaware Press
London and Toronto: Associated University Presses

Associated University Presses
440 Forsgate Drive
Cranbury, NJ 08512

Associated University Presses
25 Sicilian Avenue
London WC1A 2QH, England

Associated University Presses
2133 Royal Windsor Drive
Unit 1
Mississauga, Ontario
Canada L5J 1K5

LIBRARY OF CONGRESS CATALOGING IN PUBLICATION DATA

Lemay, J. A. Leo (Joseph A. Leo), 1935–
    New England's annoyances.

    Bibliography: p.
    Includes index.
    1. New England's annoyances.   I. New England's
annoyances.   II. Title.
ML3561.N49L4   1985   784.4'974   84-40414
ISBN 0-87413-278-9

Printed in the United States of America

For John Clarke Lemay

Contents

Preface

"New England's Annoyances" is the earliest extant American folk song—that is, the earliest song written in English in what is now the United States that descends to us anonymously and through the oral tradition. The song's survival in the oral tradition for over a century attests that it possessed extraordinary appeal for the American colonists. "New England's Annoyances" has never been the subject of any scholarly inquiry, despite being recognized both as a minor masterpiece of American humor and as an exceptionally popular early song. My interest in the poem began in 1966, when I chanced across a 1758 text radically different from any in the standard scholarly sources. I reported my find to Professors Harold S. Jantz and Harrison T. Meserole, both of whom I knew to be interested in seventeenth-century American poetry, and I had the pleasure of learning that it was, indeed, a text hitherto unknown to them. Since my newly found version contained eighteen lines not in the standard text and differed in numerous details from the other texts in the twenty-six lines it shared with them, it presented an interesting challenge. My friends Professors Jantz and Meserole agreed with me that it was a genuine folk descendent of the original song, written over a century before Benjamin Mecom printed it in 1758. By combining lines from the new text with two other texts, Professor Jantz reconstructed a version of the original. He sent copies of his reconstruction to Professor Meserole and to me, and Professor Meserole printed the reconstruction in his *Seventeenth-Century American Poetry: An Anthology* (New York: New York University Press, 1968), 503–5. I examined Professor Jantz's reconstructed version, found that I agreed with him in almost all details, and sent him my thoughts on it. Professor Jantz then urged me, in a letter of February 7, 1968, to write a "scholarly text-critical account of the whole matter." Consequently, I began making occasional notes on the song although other commitments prevented me from devoting any sustained time to the project until 1981. In 1970, while compiling a bibliography of the periodical verse of the

American Revolution, I found another version of "New England's Annoyances," which, although earlier (1774) than the supposedly first extant publication (1791) of the song, was nearly identical to that text.

Chapter 1, "Promotion Tracts and Satirical Ballads," explores the literary contexts of "New England's Annoyances." The song replies to the exaggerated promotion literature that presents New England as a semiparadise, and at the same time it satirizes the antipromotion ballads of the early seventeenth century. Indeed, at first it seems to be another antipromotion ballad, discouraging prospective emigrants to America by telling them the actual truth about New England. Chapter 2, "The Colonist's Lot: Hardships and Hindrances," deals with the song's allusions, pointing out that they create a mythical time of hardship by uniting the difficulties of different years from the 1620s to the 1640s. The allusions reveal that the song could not have been composed before the 1640s (it is usually dated 1630) and its structure and contents show that it was written in 1643, for it was evidently inspired by a promotion tract of that year, *New England's First Fruits.* Chapter 3, "The Earliest American Identities," investigates the song, demonstrating that a New Englander wrote it and that the real audience was not the prospective English emigrants whom the song directly addresses but the New Englanders who had already emigrated to the New World and who may have been tempted to remigrate. Constance Rourke and other scholars have generally thought that the hillbilly as an American character type emerged in the early nineteenth century. But the New Englanders portrayed by the folksong are clearly archetypes of the Southern moonshiner: hard-drinking, corn-eating, Dogpatch hillbillies who wear ragged, patched, and repatched clothes. "New England's Annoyances" reveals that the hillbilly is the first popularly adopted American self-characterization. This chapter also explores the religious and democratic values underlying the song and attempts to explain how and why these values emerged. Chapter 4, "Who Wrote the Song," considers which New Englander of the earliest generation could have written the song. Because of similarities of theme, tone, subject, and diction between the song and the known works of Edward Johnson, I argue that he must be the author. The appendixes consider the textual problems. The first appendix shows that the 1758 version descends from the original text. The second maintains that the 1774, 1791, and 1822 texts all derive from the same source, an anonymous lady who was evidently 94 years old in 1767. Appendix

3 proves that all nineteenth-century texts descend from the 1791 text and charts the relationships of the key texts. And appendixes 4 through 7 present the case for a reconstruction and attempt to reconstruct the original song, which is printed as the Prologue.

Winterthur Museum Library

Acknowledgments

Professor Emeritus Harold S. Jantz provided an example of a reconstructed text of "New England's Annoyances," urged me to write a detailed account of the song, suggested that Edward Johnson wrote the original, and encouraged me by his continued interest in this project. He has my gratitude, admiration, and affection.

Mr. Marcus A. McCorison, director and librarian of the American Antiquarian Society; Dr. Stephen T. Riley, former director of the Massachusetts Historical Society; Mr. Thomas R. Adams, former librarian of the John Carter Brown Library; Mr. L. D. Geller, director of the Pilgrim Society; and Professor Harrison T. Meserole have generously replied to my enquiries. My research assistants, Joseph Fireoved, Rosemary Sannini, and especially Carla Mulford, have made valuable suggestions. And I am indebted to my colleague Professor Richard L. Bushman for reading and commenting on the manuscript.

I am grateful to the Guggenheim Foundation, for I devoted some time to research on "New England's Annoyances" while I held a Guggenheim Fellowship in 1975–76; and I am grateful to President E. A. Trabant, Provost L. Leon Campbell, and the Institute for Advanced Study at the University of Delaware for supporting my research and writing during the academic year 1980–81 while I worked on this and other projects.

Prologue
"New England's Annoyances": A Reconstruction

In the appendixes I print and discuss the surviving texts of "New England's Annoyances" and step-by-step reconstruct a hypothetical version of America's first folk song. Unless new evidence turns up, I believe that the following reconstruction (which is better unified, more interesting, and more complete than the extant traditional versions) is as close as we can come to the original. Evidently composed in 1643, "New England's Annoyances" was probably printed as a broadside at the Cambridge, Massachusetts, press in that year. Although all copies of the original text have disappeared, the song survived in the oral tradition for over a century. Finally, in 1758, Benjamin Mecom (who had been trained as a printer by his uncle Benjamin Franklin) printed it as filler in a chapbook: "An Old Song, wrote *by one of our first* New England *Planters*, on *their Management in Those* good *Old* Times. *To The Tune of* a Cobler there was, etc." Other versions from a different oral tradition appeared in a newspaper of 1774, a magazine of 1791, and a newspaper of 1822. The following reconstruction is based upon these four texts. I must stress that this text is a hypothetical recreation. Accurate texts of the actual recorded song are printed below, pp. 88–89 and 91–93.

The song was sung to an old English folk tune best known by the title "Derry down." Therefore, each stanza probably concluded with a refrain similar to "Hey down, down, hey down derry down."

New England's Annoyances

1

New England's annoyances you that would know them,
Pray ponder these verses which briefly doth show them.
The place where we live is a wilderness wood,
Where grass is much wanting that's fruitful and good.

2
From the end of November till three months are gone,   5
The ground is all frozen as hard as a stone,
Our mountains and hills and vallies below,
Being commonly covered with ice and with snow.

3
And when the north-wester with violence blows,
Then every man pulls his cap over his nose;   10
But if any's so hardy and will it withstand,
He forfeits a finger, a foot, or a hand.

4
When the ground opens we then take the hoe,
And make the ground ready to plant and to sow;
Our corn being planted and seed being sown,   15
The worms destroy much before it is grown.

5
While it is growing much spoil there is made,
By birds and by squirrels that pluck up the blade;
Even when it is grown to full corn in the ear,
It's apt to be spoil'd by hog, racoon, and deer.   20

6
Our money's soon counted, for we have just none,
All that we brought with us is wasted and gone.
We buy and sell nothing but upon exchange,
Which makes all our dealings uncertain and strange.

7
And now our garments begin to grow thin,   25
And wool is much wanted to card and to spin;
If we can get a garment to cover without,
Our innermost garment is clout upon clout.

8
Our clothes we brought with us are apt to be torn,
They need to be clouted before they are worn,   30
For clouting our garments does injure us nothing:
Clouts double are warmer than single whole clothing.

9
If flesh meat be wanting to fill up our dish,
We have carrots and pumpkins and turnips and fish;
And when we have a mind for a delicate dish,   35
We repair to the clam banks, and there we catch fish.

10
Instead of pottage and puddings and custards and pies,
Our pumpkins and parsnips are common supplies;

We have pumpkin at morning and pumpkin at noon;
If it was not for pumpkins we should be undone.   40

11
If barley be wanting to make into malt,
We must be contented and think it no fault;
For we can make liquor to sweeten our lips,
Of pumpkins and parsnips and walnut tree chips.

12
And of our green corn-stalks we make our best beer,   45
We put it in barrels to drink all the year:
Yet I am as healthy, I verily think,
Who make the spring-water my commonest drink.

13
And we have a Cov'nant one with another,
Which makes a division 'twixt brother and brother: 50
For some are rejected, and others made Saints,
Of those that are equal in virtues and wants.

14
For such like annoyance we've many mad fellows
Find fault with our apples before they are mellow;
And they are for England, they will not stay here,   55
But meet with a lion in shunning a bear.

15
Now while some are going let others be coming,
For while liquor is boiling it must have a scumming;
But we will not blame them, for birds of a feather,
By seeking their fellows are flocking together.   60

16
But you who the Lord intends hither to bring,
Forsake not the honey for fear of the sting;
But bring both a quiet and contented mind,
And all needful blessings you surely shall find.

1
Promotion Tracts and Satirical Ballads

Like so much colonial American literature, "New England's Annoyances" is promotional: it opens by directly addressing the prospective emigrant who wants to know the truth about New England's disadvantages and concludes by reassuring him that he will find "all needful blessings" in New England. But it differs drastically from the usual propaganda. Writers of promotion literature wanted to lure Old World citizens to emigrate.[1] Naturally they emphasized the attractions of life in the New World. They usually exaggerated. Consequently the New World often fell short of the emigrants' expectations. Indeed, the beginnings of most colonies were filled with incredible hardships. When starvation and massacre did not threaten the early colonists, the wilderness itself was strange and forbidding to those raised in the Old World. The result was that many would-be emigrants were disappointed, returned to England, and told of their unhappy experiences. These oral tales furnished the substratum of an anti-Americanism that flourished in seventeenth- and eighteenth-century England and Europe. Further, the sceptics who mocked the reports of abundance and fertility in America continued literary traditions. Exaggerated accounts in classical times had provoked such spoofs as Lucian's *Vera Historia*. Middle Ages and Renaissance writers burlesqued travelers' tales with such satires as *The Land of Cockaygne*. So when the reports of New World fertility and abundance began circulating in England, the satirists had a ready reply. George Chapman, Ben Jonson, and John Marston, in their popular play *Eastward Hoe!* (London, 1605), lampooned the Virginia propaganda by putting a lubberland speech in the mouth of a fool aptly named Seagull.[2] Ballads appeared burlesquing the claims of the promotion writers. Other popular English songs told of the miseries and hardships of New World life. All good promotion literature had to take account of these anti-American rumors, ballads, and songs. "New En-

gland's Annoyances" uses a surprising rhetorical strategy to counteract the typical English satires of promotion literature. The song
boasts of the difficulties of New England life. Turning the tables on
the English antipromotion songs by emphasizing those very "discommodities" that promotion literature usually ignores or glosses
over, it uses the materials of the anti-American rumors as the basis
of its promotional pitch. This chapter examines the best early
American promotion literature and the extant anti-New England
songs and ballads written before 1643 in order to show how "New
England's Annoyances" reflects and responds to the promotion literature and to the satires.

Anti-American rumors existed even before Thomas Hariot
wrote *A Brief and True Report of the New Found Land of Virginia*
(1588), for Hariot claims he wrote the tract to counteract the slan-
ders and rumors concerning America. In a passage echoed by
American pioneers for the following three centuries, Hariot scoffed
at the foolish expectations of the naive, comfort-loving greenhorns:
"Some also were of a nice bringing up, only in cities or townes, or
such as never (as I may say) had seene the world before. Because
there were not to bee found any English cities, nor such faire
houses, nor at their owne wish any of their olde accumstomed
daintie food, nor any soft beds of downe or fethers; the country was
to them miserable, and their reports thereof according."[3] In his *Map
of Virginia* (1612), Captain John Smith wrote this paean to the
country: "The mildnesse of the aire, the fertility of the soile, and
the situation of the rivers are so propitious to the nature and use of
man as no place is more convenient for pleasure, profit, and mans
sustenance." But Smith too knew the rumors (and experienced the
starving times), so he followed Hariot (whose words he evidently
knew almost by heart) in castigating the malcontents' reports:

Yet some bad natures will not sticke to slander the Countrey, that will
slovenly spit at all things, especially in company where they can find
none to contradict them. Who though they were scarse ever 10 miles
from James town, or at the most but at the falles; yet holding it a great
disgrace that amongst so much action, their actions were nothing, ex-
claime of all things, though they never adventured to knowe anything;
nor ever did anything but devoure the fruits of other mens labours.
Being for most part of such tender educations and small experience in
martiall accidents, because they found not English cities, nor such faire
houses, nor at their owne wishes any of their accustomed daintes, with
feather beds and downe pillowes, Tavernes and alehouses in every
breathing place, neither such plenty of gold and silver and dissolute

liberty as they expected, had little or no care of any thing, but to pamper their bellies, to fly away with our Pinnaces, or procure their means to returne for England. For the Country was to them a miserie, a ruine, a death, a hell and their reports here, and their owne actions there according.[4]

Although the promotional writers all knew the anti-American rumors, popular oral satires, and the anti-American ballads and songs, some writers were genuinely amazed at the abundance of wildlife, fish, and various "Commodities" in the New World. Even the pilgrim fathers, in their first report from New England, stressed nature's abundance and the mild climate of Massachusetts. Edward Winslow, writing in *A Relation or Journal of the Beginning and Proceedings of the English Plantation setled at Plymouth in New England* (1622), found the winters no colder than England's, though the summers were "somewhat hotter." He conceded "some thinke it to be colder in Winter, but I cannot out of experience so say." He dwelt on the "great abundance" of the fish and fowl, adding "fresh Codd in the Summer is but course meat with us." Winslow's praise of the country concludes with this summary:

> . . . our Bay is full of Lobsters all the Summer, and affordeth variety of other Fish; in September we can take a Hogshead of Eels in a night, with small labour, and can dig them out of their beds, all the winter we have Mussells and Othus at our doores. Oysters we have none neere, but we can have them brought by the *Indians* when we will; all the Spring time the earth sendeth forth naturally very good Sallet Herbs; here are Grapes, white and red, and very sweete and strong also. Strawberies, Gooseberries, Raspas, &c.. Plums of three sorts, with blacke and red, being almost as good as a Damsen; abundance of Roses, white, red, and damask: single, but very sweet indeed; the Countrey wanteth only industrious men to imploy; for it would grieve your hearts (if as I), you had seene so many myles together by goodly Rivers uninhabited; and withal, to consider those parts of the world wherein you live to be even greatly burthened with abundance of people.[5]

In *Good News from New England* (1624), Winslow reported that the colony had suffered from the exaggerated reports of the abundance that he, William Hilton, and others had sent back. For the 1621 colonists had arrived without sufficient food, not even enough for the sailors' return voyage. After the Plymouth colonists supplied them, the pilgrims had to live "with a bare and short allowance." Winslow blamed neither the sailors nor the newcomers, "but rather" himself and "certain amongst ourselves, who were too prodigal in their writing and reporting of that plenty we enjoyed."[6] Winslow learned by hard experience not to paint too rosy a picture of the country. In the first book written from a permanent English settlement, *A True Relation of . . . Virginia* (1608), Captain John Smith had stressed that the emigrants were ignorant of the techniques necessary to sustain life in the American wilderness: "Though there be fish in the Sea, fowles in the ayre, and Beasts in the woods, their bounds are so large, they so wilde, and we so weake and ignorant, we cannot much trouble them."[7] And in his *Description of New England* (1616), Smith, after a long catalogue of the superabounding plenty offered in America, warned the possible emigrant, "all which are to be had in abundance observing but their seasons. But if a man will goe at Christmasse to gather Cherries in *Kent*, he may be deceived, though there be plentie in summer: so heere, these plenties have each their season."[8] And Winslow, in *Good News*, shows that he had profited by Smith's literary example: "I will not again speak of the abundance of fowl, store of venison, and variety of fish, in their seasons, which might encourage many to go in their persons. Only I advise all such beforehand to consider, that as they hear of countries that abound with the good creatures of God, so means must be used for the taking of every one in his kind, and therefore not only to content themselves that there is sufficient, but to foresee how they shall be able to obtain the same." Winslow then proves that he was the right person for the pilgrims to choose as their promoter, for he convinces the reader with a logical comparison: "Otherwise, as he that walketh London streets, though he be in the midst of plenty, yet if he want means, is not the better, but hath rather his sorrow increased by the sight of that he wanteth, and cannot enjoy it, so also there, if thou want art and other neccessaries thereunto belonging, thou mayest see that thou wantest and thy heart desireth, and yet be never the better for the same." And Winslow concludes his appeal with an attack on the malcontents who have returned to England to spread rumors (and truths) about the hard life and starving times in Plymouth Colony:

> I write not these things to dissuade any that shall seriously, upon due examination, set themselves to further the glory of God, and the honor of our country, in so worthy an enterprise, but rather to discourage such as with too great lightness undertake such courses; who peradventure strain themselves and their friends for their passage thither, and

are no sooner there, than seeing their foolish imagination made void, are at their wits' end, and would give ten times so much for their return, if they could procure it; and out of such discontented passions and humors, spare not to lay that imputation upon the country, and others, which themselves deserve.[9]

Captain Christopher Levett, like Smith, had a commonsensical and realistic tone. Knowing the dangers of promotion literature, he directly claimed that his own tract, *A Voyage into New England* (1628), took the middle course, "for my desire is, that the saddle may be set on the right horse, and the ass may be rid, and the knave punished either for discouraging or encouraging to much, whosoever he bee."[10] Levett, like John Hammond in 1656 and Benjamin Franklin in 1782,[11] attempted to disarm his possible critics by directly—and humorously—referring to the lubberland burlesques. He begins the chapter on the country's "Commodities and Discommodities" by writing his own spoof of the exaggerations:

I will not do therein as some have done to my knowledge, speak more than is true: I will not tell you that you may smell the corn fields before you see the land; neither must men think that corn doth grow naturally, (or on trees) nor will the deer come when they are called, or stand still and look on a man until he shoot him, not knowing a man from a beast; nor the fish leap into the kittle, nor on the dry land, neither are they so plentiful, that you may dip them up in baskets, nor take cod in nets to make a voyage, which is no truer than that the fowls will present themselves to you with spits through them.[12]

Despite the lessons of the best promotion writers and despite the English satires, the naifs would not learn. The Reverend Francis Higginson, coming over in the vanguard of the Massachusetts Bay Colony, wrote his friend in England a description that anachronistically sounds as if Captain Levett had it in mind when he abused the knaves who exaggerated American conditions:

We saw many schools of mackerel, infinite multitudes on every side of our ship. The sea was abundantly stored with rockweed and yellow flowers like gillyflowers. By noon we were within three leagues of Capan [Cape Ann], and as we sailed along the coasts we saw every hill and dale and every island full of gay woods and high trees. The nearer we came to the shore the more flowers in abundance, sometimes scattered abroad, sometimes joined in sheets nine or ten yards long, which we supposed to be brought from the low meadows by the tide. Now what with fine woods and green trees by land and these yellow flowers painting the sea, [it] made us all desirous to see our new paradise of New England.[13]

Higginson's promotion tract *New-Englands Plantation* (1630) continued the same strain, celebrating the New World fertility and abundance, although he did mention four "discommodities": mosquitoes, the cold, snakes, and the lack of other "good . . . honest Christians."[14] Another early emigrant, John (?) Pond, sent back an honest report to his father, asking for provisions and telling of the greenhorn's dilemma: "Here is good store of fish, if we had boats to go eight or ten leagues to sea to fish in. Here are good store of wild fowl, but they are hard to come by. It is harder to get a shot than it is in ould eingland."[15]

Thomas Dudley, Anne Bradstreet's father, wrote a realistic report, which, since he had "no table nor other room to write in than by the fireside upon my knee in this sharp winter," begins on a sure note of discomfort and hardship. He twice complains of the "too large commendations of the country" sent back by Higginson and others in 1629. He explains that he "more willingly" writes such an "open and plain" manner, "lest other men should fall short of their expectations when they come hither, as we to our great prejudice did, by means of letters sent us from hence into England, wherein honest men out of a desire to draw over others to them wrote somewhat hyperbolically of many things here." Despite his reservations, Dudley hits the true Puritan note when he castigates the "malcontents" who "have raised many false and scandalous reports against us." Those sloths returned to England because they did not see "other means than by their labor to feed themselves." He assures his readers that if they want to emigrate for spiritual reasons, they "may find here what may well content" them: "Materials to build, fuel to burn, ground to plant, seas and rivers to fish in, a pure air to breath in, good water to drink till wine or beer can be made, which, together with the cows, hogs, and goats brought hither already, may suffice for food, for as for fowl and venison, they are dainties here as well as in England."[16]

Captain John Smith's last book, *Advertisements for the unexperienced Planters of New England* (1631), discussed the Massachusetts Bay Colony. Smith said that John Winthrop allowed "Some two hundred" weak-hearted malcontents "to returne for *England*, whose clamors are as variable as their humours and Auditors. Some say they could see no timber of two feet diameter, some the Country is all Woods; others they drunke all the Springs and Ponds dry, yet like to famish for want of fresh water; some of the danger of the rattell Snake; and that others sold their provisions at what rates they pleased to them that wanted, and so returned to *England* great gainers out of others miseries; yet all that returned are not of those humors." And, again following Hariot, he heaped scorn upon those fools who expected "to finde amongst those salvages such Churches, Palaces, Monuments, and Buildings as are in *England*."[17] In one of the best New England promotion tracts, William Wood justified *New England's Prospect* (1634) as an antidote to the "imperfect" relations already published and "also because there hath been many scandalous and false reports past upon the country, even from the sulphurious breath of every base ballad-monger."

Thus, like writers of promotion literature from at least Hariot's time, Wood calls attention to the anti-American popular subculture of Renaissance and seventeenth-century England. Although he is the first writer to mention the anti-American ballads, they had already (as I shall show below) existed for some time. Like many of his predecessors, Wood mocks the naiveté of those who were disappointed by the fledgling American settlements: "I have myself heard some say that they heard it was a rich land, a brave country, but when they came there they could see nothing but a few Canvis Boothes and old houses, supposing at the first to have found walled townes, fortifications and corne fields, as if townes could have built themselves, without the husbandrie of man. These men missing of their expectations returned home and railed against the Country."[18] Wood probably had a specific anti-American ballad in mind when he wrote this criticism, for a popular anti-American song, "A West-Country Man's Voyage to New England," contains the following stanza:

> When first che did land che mazed me quite
> And 'twas of all daies on Satterday night,
> Che wondred to see the strong building were there,
> 'Twas all like the standing at *Bartholomew* Fair.[19]

Whether or not Wood was replying to the specific criticism of a particular ballad, there can be no doubt that he, like Hariot, Smith, Levett, Winslow, and other promotional writers, was aware of the criticisms. And like the other writers, Wood knew the anti-American ballads. So did the author of "New England's Annoyances." The song should be seen not only in the context of American promotion literature and the satires of America by English dramatists and oral anecdotalists, but especially against the background of those productions that came from "the sulphurious breath of every base ballad-monger."

No doubt many early ballads satirizing America have been lost.[20] Most extant ones are reprints. Few are dated. And the authors are usually unknown. Nevertheless, at least the following six songs satirizing New England evidently circulated before 1643; and all but the first attained popularity. The earliest song satirizing puritan emigrants is an anonymous and untitled ballad, dating from about 1615, which survives only in a commonplace book. The 112-line poem begins:

> In England there is no hope to staye
> where good men are displaced
> To Amsterdam is your onlye waie
> and there we shall be graced[21]

The opening couplet echoes a commonplace sentiment usually attributed to a fool or a personified vice. I doubt that the song was popular in the oral tradition, for it is quite scholarly, mentioning the Puritans' overthrowing "the Stagerite" to follow the logic of "Peeter Ramus." Despite its ballad meter of alternating iambic tetrameters and trimeters, the refrain (or rather, what I judge to be the refrain) suggests that the song was sung to a "Derry Down" variant: "Ha downe downe heighe downe / my brethren staye not heere." As Bertrand H. Bronson makes clear in his notes to the music of "King John and the Bishop" (Child No. 45), a variety of folk tunes could be used even for the anapestic tetrameter couplet; and a legion of possibilities was available for the ballad meter.[22]

The most popular anti-New England ballad appeared about 1629. One untitled version was written on the back of a will dated 2 May 1631.[23] Since this version differs from the several others extant, I believe that the ballad had already passed into the folk tradition by 1631. Evidently the original title was "A Proper New Ballet Called the Summons to Newe England." Although the ballad was to be sung "to the tune of the townesmens cappe," I have not been able to find the tune.[24] The earliest printed text I have encountered appeared in 1661 under the title "New England Described."[25] Although most versions of the song begin "Let all the purifidean ["putrifidean" or "Purisidean" or "fratrisedian" or "parisidean"] Sect," the 1661 text opens:

Among the purifidian Sect,
I mean the counterfeit Elect:
Zealous bankrupts, Punks devout,
Preachers suspended, rabble rout,
Let them sell all, and out of hand
Prepare to go to *New England*,
    To build new *Bable* strong and sure,
    Now call'd a Church unspotted pure.

Stanzas 2 through 6 satirize the glowing reports of American fertility. These lines echo the lubberland tradition common in English and European satire, and, indeed, present in at least one Restoration ballad, *An Invitation to Lubberland* (1685).[26] Here is the second stanza of "New England Described":

There Milk from Springs, like Rivers, flows,
And Honey upon hawthorn grows;
Hemp, Wool, and Flax, there grows on trees,
The mould is fat, it cuts like cheese;
All fruits and herbs spring in the fields,
Tobacco it good plenty yields;
    And there shall be a Church most pure,
    Where you may find salvation sure.

Stanzas 7 through 10 continue the satire on the Puritans begun in the first stanza, a generalized satire common throughout the period, with glances at the Puritans' supposed practice of free love and absolute democracy—even anarchy—in the social order.[27] The song's concluding stanza bids good riddance to the emigrants:

Let Amsterdam send forth her Brats,
Her Fugitives and Runnagates:
Let Bedlam, Newgate, and the Clink
Disgorge themselves unto this sink;
Let Bridewell and the stews be swept,
And all sent hither to be kept,
    So may our Church be cleans'd and pure
    Keep both it self and state secure.

A professional ballad writer probably composed this song. It does not seem to reflect actual experience. It brings up the topics of seventeenth-century antipuritan satire, adding one inaccurate (for New England in the 1630s) reference to tobacco.

A third anti-New England song, usually titled "The Zealous

Puritan," is probably the ballad entered in the Stationers' Register on 20 March 1638/9, where it is called "A Friendly Invitation to a New Plantation."[28] It is possible, however, that "A Friendly Invitation" was a straightforward promotion song and that "The Zealous Puritan" burlesques it. Comparable nineteenth-century promotion songs were sometimes superseded in the oral tradition by satires upon them.[29] Here is its first stanza:

> My Brethren all attend,
> And list to my relation:
> This is the day, mark what I say,
> Tends to your renovation;
> Stay not among the Wicked
> Lest that with them you perish,
> But let us to *New-England* go,
> And the Pagan People cherish;
>> *Then for the truths sake come along, come along,*
>> *Leave this place of Superstition:*
>> *Were it not for we, that the Brethren be,*
>> *You would sink into Perdition.*[30]

Like most other antipromotion ballads, "A Friendly Invitation" contains no details of American experience. It satirizes puritan religious practice and supposed hypocrisy, viewing America as a place free from bishops and spiritual courts and outside "The Laws controulment." Its tune was "Tom a Bedlam."[31]

Entered in the Stationers' Register of licensed publications by Richard Harper on 19 June 1640,[32] the song "And is not Old England grown New" first appeared in two songbooks in 1661. By then, it had passed into the oral tradition, for the two texts are quite different.[33] Here is the first stanza:

> You talk of *New-England*, I truely believe
> Old *England* is grown new, and doth us deceive
> I'll ask you a question or two, by your leave,
>> And is not old *England* grown new?[34]

This song catalogues the changing conditions of England, implies that all changes are for the worse, and finds them characteristic of New England. (Blaming Europe's changes on its "Americanization" is nothing new.) Like the other anti-New England songs, it contains no American details. Its tune was the "Blacksmith," a popular melody familiar today as "Greensleeves."[35]

A song satirizing the puritan leaders of Parliament for sup-posedly wanting to emigrate appeared about 1640.[36] John Pym and John Hampden were patentees of Connecticut; both were inter-ested in New England; and rumor frequently reported their plans for emigration.[37] Since they both died in 1643, it seems unlikely that a song satirizing them would have been written after that date. It is simply entitled "A Song." Here is the first stanza as printed in the *Rump* (1662):

> *New-England* is preparing a-pace,
> To entertain King *Pym*, with his Grace,
> And *Isaack* before shall carry the Mace,
>   *For Round-heads Old Nick stand up now.*[38]

Like the others, this song contains no American details. It is merely an antipuritan satire. A manuscript version at the Huntington Li-brary says that it is "To the tune of Come buy my new Almanack, new."[39] Although I do not know this tune, and although it would be possible to sing the song to "Derry down," I suspect that it, like "*Old* England *turned* New," was sung to the tune of "The Black-smith" or "Greensleeves."

The only English ballad about New England that reflects some knowledge of the American experience (probably from the oral rumors) is the one I believe William Wood had in mind in 1634, sometimes entitled "The New England Ballad" and sometimes "A West-Country Man's Voyage to New England."[40] The song prob-ably dates from about 1633, although the earliest extant version is in a songbook printed in 1661. Charles H. Firth said, "As Dorches-ter was one of the oldest towns in Massachusetts, it [the song] may have been written twenty years or more before the date of its publication [1661]."[41] An examination of the ballad will document the common satirical jibes about New England and may also help to date the song.

The first stanza introduces the persona, a "West Country man" (i.e., in the popular literature of the day, a bumpkin who spoke in a rude dialect)[42] who emigrated to New England, was disappointed at what he found there, and returned to England:

> My Masters give audience, and listen to me,
> And straight che will tell you where che have be:
> Che have been in *New-England*, but now cham come o'er,
> Itch do think they shal catch me go thither no more.

The second stanza satirizes the Edenic and cornucopia motifs of American promotional literature. The naif believed the tales of America's abundance and fertility—but found them all lies. The next stanza describes the speaker's landing in America on a Saturday night (a time associated with revels and a natural time to visit the fairs). He ironically says that he was surprised to see "the strong buildings," which were like those at "Bartholomew Fair,"[43] thus condemning the structures as tents and frame shacks. The next morning the bumpkin was disappointed "to hear no Bells chime" and learned that it was because "they had never a Bell in the Town." Since England prided itself on being "the ringing island,"[44] this may have been a meaningful contemporary criticism. Stanzas 5 through 8 satirize the supposed Puritan church services. The author appeals to the Anglicans' prejudice by suggesting that the Massachusetts Puritans did not believe in a learned ministry. The immigrant went to the church expecting to "hear some prayer," but found that the minister did not "teach," since "They scorn'd to pray, they were all able to preach." This criticism may reflect English complaints that Plymouth Colony lacked a minister.[45] Robert Cushman's *A Sermon Preached at Plimouth in New England Dec. 9, 1622* (London, 1622/3) provides an example of the Plymouth Puritans' lay preaching, and William Rathband, in *A Brief Narration of Some Church Courses in New England* (1644) condemned Cushman's sermon as one "made there by a comber of wool."[46] Further, when Edward Winslow returned to England, he was prosecuted for preaching at Plymouth.[47] Nevertheless, the Plymouth colonists definitely believed in a learned ministry. The charge was also false for Dorchester, Massachusetts, where the immigrant had supposedly landed. The Dorchester church was organized in Plymouth, England, before the emigrants sailed, with the Reverend John Maverick as teacher and the Reverend John Warham as pastor. It was New England's second established church, preceded only by Salem.[48]

Stanza 6 criticizes the Puritans for using a different psalm book— "They had got a new Song to the tune of the same." This could refer to the *Bay Psalm Book*, which would date the ballad after 1640, but the Plymouth Puritans began replacing the usual Anglican version (by Sternhold and Hopkins) with Henry Ainsworth's *The Book of Psalms* (Amsterdam: Giles Thorp, 1612) immediately after its publication.[49] The Salem group officially adopted the Ainsworth psalter. Since Ainsworth wrote in his edition that he had taken "most" of the tunes from "our former English Psalms, where they will fit the measure of the verse," the criticism in stanza 6 (even if it is accurate) probably refers to the Ainsworth psalter, which was frequently reprinted in the seventeenth century.[50] Besides, references to Puritan hymns and psalms abounded in anti-Puritan satires of the seventeenth century.[51] They occur, for instance, in "A Friendly Invitation to a New Plantation" where the prospective emigrant is told: "There you may teach our hymns, / Without the Laws controulment"; and "the Psalms shall be our Musick."[52]

Stanza 7 satirizes adult baptism ("a child . . . About sixteen years old"), the lack of godparents, and the teenager's supposed usurpation of authority: "The Priest durst not cross him for fear of his ill will." Needless to say, these criticisms simply reflect the common topics of satire.[53] Stanzas 8 and 9 also describe New England church practice. The "next day" our bumpkin attended his friend's wedding, where he saw a magistrate—rather than a minister— marry the couple. This, of course, reflects the actual practice of Plymouth and of the Massachusetts Bay Colony and does not help date the song.[54] The speaker also reports that no ring was used in the service and that the woman was not given away by anyone. These charges echo the "free love" criticism commonly used to put down Puritans.[55]

Stanzas 10 through 12 conclude the poem. Stanza 10 locates the action in "new Dorchester," a town "very famous in all that Country." If the ballad were composed by a ballad-maker and is not based on an emigrant's actual experience, then the selection of Dorchester as the scene makes sense only if the ballad were written well before 1640. Although the ballad could refer to the Dorchester Company, which was known for its Gloucester, Massachusetts, colony in the 1620s, the settlement failed in 1624 and most of the emigrants returned to England.[56] The ballad probably refers to Dorchester, Massachusetts, which was, according to William Wood in 1634, "the greatest Towne in *New-England*."[57] But by the late 1630s, Boston had far surpassed Dorchester in size and fame. I doubt that any ballad-maker would set his action in Dorchester after 1640, for by then Boston had become synonymous with Puritan New England. Even if the ballad were written by someone who actually emigrated to America (an unlikely possibility, for the ballad reflects the satirical traditions expertly), its subject was probably the initial 1629–32 settlement at Dorchester, Massachusetts. After 1635, one could hardly say that Dorchester "'twas new building." By then, it was among the colony's older towns, and the newer ones, especially Boston, were booming.[58]

The bumpkin-persona stays in Dorchester "till che was weary at heart," but finds when he "got leave to depart" that he "had three-score shillings for swearing to pay." This suggests a well-established church and rules, typical of the late 1630s and thereafter; but, once again, such laws are a common motif in antipuritan literature[59] and mention of them does not help date the poem. In the final stanza, the immigrant swears one more oath, that he "would stay no more longer to swear on the score." He concludes by bidding farewell to New England's "Fowlers and Fishers" (another unrealistic note, for most New Englanders—and certainly those at Dorchester—were preponderantly farmers). The historical evidence concerning New England in the ballad suggests a date of composition between 1631 and 1636. Further, the antipuritan satire within the work makes it much more likely to be a creation of the Royalist 1630s than the Puritan Interregnum. I suspect that this anonymous[60] ballad was composed by a professional ballad writer around 1632 and that William Wood had it particularly in mind in 1634 when he referred to the "many scandalous and false reports past upon the country, even from the sulphurious breath of every base ballad-monger."

Such are the major promotion tracts and the surviving anti-New England ballads of the early seventeenth century. In reply, "New England's Annoyances" not only burlesques the exaggerated portraits of American abundance that characterize the promotion literature, it also satirizes the lubberland motif common in the anti-American ballads.[61] Colonial promotion literature is responsible for the creation of that major theme in American literature, the American Dream. In effect, the antipromotion ballads mock a material and degenerate version of the American Dream. But the American Dream takes numerous forms. Its fundamental characteristic is the dream of possibility: that a person may change, may achieve extraordinary accomplishments, may learn to know himself, may create a better society or a better world. That hope, that possibility, usually demands a seeming innocence, a naïveté. So the American is often a naïf—or, rather, like Benjamin Franklin in his *Autobiography*, a character who *pretends* to be naive. Since versions of the American Dream are so common in American literature and culture, disenchantment and mocking replies also characterize its literature and culture. But the best satires on the American Dream, like

Thoreau's *Walden* and Fitzgerald's *The Great Gatsby*, are not only satires. They go on to create their own versions of the American Dream. "New England's Annoyances" records the earliest American pioneers' disenchantment with the realities of "God's country."[62] And, like the later great satires on the American Dream, it contains (as we shall see) its own extraordinary underlying vision.

2

The Colonist's Lot: Hardships and Hindrances

All the song's annoyances appear frequently in early New England literature. Usually they are called "discommodities," but at least William Wood (1634) and Thomas Lechford (1642) label them "annoyances."[1] Although every promotion tract that tried to give an honest report listed some disadvantages, no other writing featured as many complaints as the song. Indeed, some annoyances in the song (like the shortage of food) were true only for certain times in the colonists' experience, while others (like the cold winters) were complaints that recurred nearly every year. This chapter investigates the general validity of the song and tries to assign definite dates to specific "annoyances." Thus, in addition to supplying a historical context, I shall be compiling clues for the song's date of composition. In concluding the chapter, I shall attempt to prove that the song's major source was a well-known Massachusetts promotion tract, *New Englands First Fruits*, and that "New England's Annoyances" was composed in 1643.

The song's first complaint concerns New England's "wilderness wood" and lack of good grass (all references are to the reconstructed version). These were common grievances. In their promotion tracts, Francis Higginson (1629 and 1630), Captain John Smith (1612 and 1631), and William Wood (1634) all attempt to refute the rumor that "the Country is all Woods." Wood explained, "it is generally conceived that the woods grow so thick that there is no more clear ground than is hewed out by labor of man." He claimed, however, that "grassy valleys" were plentiful.[2] Wood also reported the complaint "that the grass grows not in those places where it was cut the foregoing years." Another writer said in 1637 that after the virgin land had been used for crops for "five or six years, it grows barren beyond belief." Although English soil, after similar use, "proves fertile for grass," the soil of New England "yields none at all, but, like the land around Dunstable, puts on the face of winter in the time of summer."[3] The song agreed that "grass is much wanting that's fruitful and good." Denials by the promotion writers proved the frequency of the charge. In 1624 William Bradford replied, "It is hear (as in all places) some better and some worse; and if they [who complain "the ground is barren and doth bear no grasse"] will consider their woods, in England they shall not find such grasse in them, as in their fields and meadows." William Wood commonsensically said: "And whereas it hath been reported that some hath mown a day for half a load of hay, I do not say, but it may be true. A man may do as much and get as little in England on Salisbury Plain or in other places where grass cannot be expected. So hay ground is not in all places in New England."[4]

The song's first sustained topic characterizes New England's severe winters (stanzas 2 and 3). Practically every early writer (after the Pilgrim Fathers, who experienced an unseasonably mild winter in 1620–21) comments on the bitter cold: Captain Christopher Levett (1628), John White (1630), Francis Higginson (1630), Thomas Dudley (1631), Captain John Smith (1631), William Wood (1634), Thomas Morton (1637), Thomas Lechford (1642), Roger Williams (1643), and Henry Dunster (1643), among others. "New England's Annoyances" echos the common complaints. The song says that for "three months," New England is "commonly covered with ice and with snow."[5] The song claims that the "north-wester" brings such weather that anyone who withstands it "forfeits a finger, a foot, or a hand." Roger Williams explains that New England is colder than England because England is an island and islands are warmer than continents; so in New England "The *Nor West* wind (which occasioneth *New-England* cold) comes over the cold frozen Land." Similarly, Wood (1634) writes that "the north west wind . . . is the cause of extreme cold weather . . . commanding every man to his house, forbidding any to out face him without prejudice to their noses . . . some venturing too nakedly in extremity of cold, being more foolhardy than wise, have for a time lost the use of their feet, others the use of their fingers." Lechford (1642) also comments that some "lose their fingers or toes every year."[6]

No early New England writers comment at length on the difficulties of raising corn (stanzas 4 and 5), perhaps partly because their English audience knew nothing about that favorite American dish. Nevertheless, Winslow (1624), Wood (1634), Morton (1637), and Johnson (1654) all mention it.[7] The song emphasizes the lack of implements since the New Englanders "take the hoe," rather than a plow, to till the fields. But the hoe continued to be the commonest implement, especially among the poor farmers, until late in the seventeenth century. Plows were scarce enough in 1636 for Winthrop to remark that "about thirty ploughs were at work." And John Winthrop, Jr., writing in 1662, said: "The Manner of planting every kind of this Corne, is in Rowes at equall distance every way about five or Six foote asunder, they open the Earth with a How, taking away the Superfices three or fower Inches deepe and the breadth of the How which is used." Since the trees were killed but left standing in the fields and since the corn was hilled, the plough may have been less practical than the hoe. Although Peter Kalm comments in the mid-eighteenth century that the plow had replaced the hoe in weeding between the rows of corn, his observations probably reflect the practice in the Middle Colonies rather than in hilly New England.[8]

The song also complains of the "spoil" made by American wildlife while the corn is growing, and historical records document these annoyances. Winslow reveals that wolves tried to eat the fish with which the Puritan Fathers fertilized the corn. Wood (1634) discusses the ravages by turkeys and especially by "stares" (probably the red-winged blackbird): "The stares be bigger than those in England, as black as crows, being the most troublesome and injurious bird of all others, pulling up the corns by the roots when it is young so that those who plant by reedy and seggy places, where they frequent, are much annoyed with them, they being so audacious that they fear not guns or their fellows hung upon poles." Morton (1637) says crows "sometimes eate our corne, and doe pay for their presumption well enough; and serveth there in powther, with turnips, to supply the place of powthered beefe." He specifically complains that crows "eatheth the Indian maisze." Winthrop recorded in 1642, "the pigeons came in such flocks (above 10,000 in one flock) that beat down, and eat up a very great quantity of all sorts of English grain." The common jay is sometimes called a "cornbird," and both the bluejay and the red-winged blackbird are called "cornthief." John Winthrop, Jr. (1662), says that "crowes or Birds" usually get some of the grains put into the ground, and that later the "strong thick huskes" of the corn "defends it from the Crowes, Sterlings, and other Birds, which would otherwise devour whole fields of it before it could come to its full maturity."

By the midseventeenth-century, several Massachusetts towns offered bounties for jays, crows, red-winged blackbirds, and other corneaters. (Some things never change. A twentieth-century folk rhyme on the planting of corn says "One for the blackbird, one for the crow, / One for the cutworm, and one to grow.") Wood mentions a kind of squirrel "which doth much trouble the planters of corn, so that they are constrained to set diverse traps and to carry their cats into the corn fields till their corn be three weeks old." Evidently Wood had the Eastern chipmunk in mind, for John Winthrop, Jr., says some grains of newly planted corn are "plucked up" by "Mouse-Squirrels (a little creature, that doth much hurt in some Fields newly planted)." Morton (1637) claims that red squirrels even try to get corn after harvest: "hee haunts our howses and will rob us of our Corne." In the mideighteenth century, Peter Kalm testified that corn had more enemies than any other grain "from the time it begins to ripen and even after it is stored."[9] In the late eighteenth century, William Bartram described the Georgia Indians dealing with problems similar to those of the early Massachusetts settlers: "The youth are daily stationed in their fields . . . to chase away crows, jackdaws, black-birds and such predatory animals . . . squirrles, birds, etc. The men in turn patrole the cornfields at night, to protect their provisions from the depredations of night rovers, as bears, racoons and deer."[10]

Stanza 6 laments the currency shortage, since "All that we bought with us is wasted and gone." Consequently the New Englanders "buy and sell nothing but upon exchange." I have not found that any writer in the 1630s comments on this problem—probably because it hardly existed as long as the emigrants to Massachusetts were continually bringing additional cash. But when emigration slowed, a depression struck and currency became scarce. On 27 June 1640, Edward Winslow wrote John Winthrop "how easie a thing it is" in England "to turne any valuable commodity into money, but it is otherwise heer, and especially at this the most hard and dead time of all other these many years." On 7 October 1640, the General Court, because of the "great stop in trade and commerce for want of money," ordered "any debt, legacy, fine, or any other payment" payable "in corne, cattle, fish, or other commodities, at such rates as this Courte shall set downe." John Winthrop first commented on the currency shortage in December 1640. John Endecott wrote Winthrop in February 1641/2 that "scarcitie of money" was "alreadie a manifest cause of debarring most" prospective emigrants from coming to New England. The first printed account to mention the shortage was Thomas Lechford's *Plain Dealing* (1642): "Money is wanting, by reason of the failing of passengers these two last yeares."[11] Henry Dunster (1643), answering the objection "You have no money there," said, "We can trade amongst ourselves by way of exchange, one commodity for another, and so doe usually." And Nathaniel Ward's *Simple Cobler of Aggawam* (1647) obliquely refers to the lack of money with a phrase that has a proverbial ring: "Time hath neither Politicks nor Ethics, good nor evill in it; it is an empty thing, as empty as a *New English* purse, and emptier it cannot bee." These quotations (and the economic history of early Massachusetts) all suggest that this stanza would not have been written before 1640, for until then "the yearly access of new Commers" supplied New England with sufficient currency.[12]

Stanzas 7 and 8 concern the wearing-out of clothing and the lack of wool and of new clothes. This is a common subject of private correspondence until about 1660. John Pond wrote on 15 March 1630/1, "here is not cloth to be had to make no [i.e., new?] apparel." Winthrop warned his son in 1631 to be sure to bring over clothing. William Wood, in *New England's Prospect* (1634), also said that everyone should "carry over good store of apparel; for if he come to buy it there, he shall find it dearer than in England." During the early explorations of Maryland, a group of servant women were returning from washing clothes when their small boat overturned with "the losse of much linnen." The Jesuit Andrew White thought this domestic disaster sufficiently important to record it in *The Relation of the Successful Beginnings of Maryland* (1634), adding ruefully "and among the rest I lost the best of mine, which is a very maine losse in these parts." Despite being more costly, clothes were available in Boston as long as money was plentiful. Indeed, to the disgust of some New Englanders, their neighbors followed the costly new European fashions too closely. At the end of September 1638 John Winthrop recorded:

> The court, taking into consideration the great disorder general through the country in costliness of apparel, and following new fashions, sent for the elders of the churches, and conferred with them about it, and laid it upon them, as belonging to them, to redress it, by urging upon the consciences of their people which they promised to do. But little was done about it; for divers of the elders' wives, etc., were in some measure partners in this general disorder.

Winthrop also said in March of 1640 that "supply of clothes and other necessaries" was more abundant in Massachusetts than in Virginia or the West Indies: "those countries (for all their great wealth) have sent hither, both this year and formerly" for these commodities. But by 1641 conditions had worsened in New England so that one reason the commissioners went to England was "to seek out some way, by procuring cotton from the West Indies" to remedy the lack of a "present supply of clothing." Lechford reported that New Englanders "want help to goe forward, for their subsistence in regard to cloathing." Thomas Weld felt he must answer the objection that "You are like to want clothes hereafter." And Thomas Hooker, writing in the early 1640s, said that "Planters, if they can provide cloth to go warm, they leave the cutts and lace to those that study to go fine." An anti-Virginia ballad suggests that lack of ready clothing was common throughout America. "The Cloaths that I brought in they are worn very thin, / In the land of Virginny, O."[13]

Although clothing was in short supply and comparatively expensive in New England throughout the early period, its shortage was more severe in the early 1640s than at any other time. William Hubbard, who graduated from Harvard in 1642, said that when the emigration stopped in 1640, "The country of New England was to seek of a way to provide themselves of clothing, which they could not attain by selling of their cattle as before; . . . to help . . . the General Court made several orders for the manufacture of woolen and linen cloth; which . . . in a little time stopped this gap in part." The one possible bit of evidence to the contrary is Nathaniel Ward's witty condemnation of women for too closely following the Court's changing fashions. But his generalized complaint in *The Simple Cobler* (1647) evidently concerns English women and a perennial fault, rather than Massachusetts and a peculiarly local failing. The earliest colonists did not make their own clothing because they had no wool. Wolves killed the sheep. But the currency shortage in the early 1640s made the colonists confront the problem. Rhode Islanders realized that by a determined effort, they could kill off all the wolves on the islands. In 1642, Aquidneck was free of wolves and, consequently, the sheep there doubled every year. By 1645, Dr. Robert Child reported that Rhode Island had nearly a thousand sheep. And as the frontier was pushed back, the coastal settlements became comparatively free of wolves. By the 1650s, sheep were becoming relatively plentiful even in Massachusetts. William Bradford, in 1654, wrote:

> But now most begin to get store of sheep,
> That, with their wool, their bodies may be clad,
> In time of straits, when things cannot be had;

> For merchants keep the price of cloth so high,
> As many are not able the same to buy.
> And happy would it be, for the people here,
> If they could raise cloth, for themselves to wear.

In the late 1650s, Rowley, Massachusetts, became famous for clothmaking. Samuel Maverick said that the inhabitants "drive a pretty trade, making Cloath and Ruggs for Cotton Wool, and also Sheeps wool with which in a few yeares the Country will abound not only to supply themselves but also to send abroad." In 1661, it was estimated that New Englanders had nearly 100,000 sheep, so much, officials feared, that English clothing was no longer necessary for them.[14] The information within stanzas 7 and 8 of "New England's Annoyances" seems by itself to date the poem between a time several years after the emigration to Massachusetts (1630s) and a period no more than ten years later (1640s), since the clothes the emigrants "brought with us" (1630 to 1638) have by now worn "thin"; many have been "torn"; and the innermost garment has been mended so often that it is patch upon patch.

New England's food (stanzas 9 and 10) is a common subject of the promotion tracts. In 1629, Higginson found "Our turnips, parsnips, and carrots are here both bigger and sweeter than is ordinarily to be found in England. Here are also store of pumpions." William Wood, in *New England's Prospect* (1634), claimed that "The ground affords very good kitchen gardens for turnips, parsnips, carrots, radishes, and pumpions." And in the same year, John Winthrop, writing to Sir Nathaniel Rich, assured him that "all sorts of rootes pumpin and other fruits" grew well, "which for tast and wholesomeness far excede those in England."[15] Bradford, in a retrospective poem of 1654, said "All sorts of roots and herbs in garden grow: / Parsnips, carrots, turnips, or what you'll sow." In 1648, Edward Johnson was especially impressed with the abundance of pumpkins: "See you that garden-plat inclos'd, Pumkins there hundreds are, / Parsnips and Roots, with Cabiges, grow in great plenty there." And the early writers, from Brereton (1602), Rosier (1605), and Smith (1616, 1620, 1622, and 1631), to Wood (1634) and others, all comment on the abundant supply of fish and shellfish.[16] In contrast to the promotion tracts, these two stanzas dwell upon the scarcity of English foods and the necessity for repetitiously eating the same American ones: "we have pumpkin at morning and pumpkin at noon; / If it was not for pumpkins we should be undone." Traditional English foods were scarce only in the 1620s (especially the early 1620s) and in the early 1630s, when new emigrants first arrived. The emigrants began to grow the traditional English foods (along with the native American corn and pumpkins) almost as soon as they began farming in America. Bradford, writing in 1646, says that after the harvest of 1623 "generall want or famine hath not been amongst them since to this day." They exported considerable food in some years during the 1630s and had a great abundance in the late 1630s.[17] Thus the historical time of scarcity depicted in stanzas 9 and 10 (the early 1620s or early 1630s) contradicts the later dates of composition suggested by stanzas 6 (on currency) and 7 and 8 (on clothing).

Stanzas 11 and 12 concern New England's drinks—liquor, beer, and water. Since English and European water was often polluted, people did not commonly drink it. The usual English drink was small beer. Water was considered, in general, an unhealthy drink. But American water was different. The quantity and quality of New England water became an important topic for almost all New England writers. Bradford says that one objection made against the Puritans' proposed move to America was that "the change of aire, diate, and drinking of water, would infecte their bodies with sore sickneses, and greevous diseases." So the promotion writers tried to reassure prospective emigrants. Captain John Smith, William Bradford, and William Wood, among others, praise the water. In a long discussion, Wood says that New England's "sweet waters" are better than the Old World's: "It is thought there can be no better water in the world. Yet dare I not prefer it before good beer as some have done, but any man will choose it before bad beer, whey, or buttermilk."[18] The early colonists continued to regard beer as more healthful. Martha Lyon (who had emigrated to New England in 1631) wrote John Winthrop in 1648/9 that she was ill, but her husband did "what he can for me . . . for he drinks water that I might drink bere." One anti-Virginia ballad voices the traditional preference: "Instead of drinking Beer, I drink the water clear, / In the Land of Virginny, O; / Which makes me pale and wan."

In "New England's Annoyances," the most striking fact about the description of drinks is the emphasis upon the worst makeshift possibilities for making liquor and beer. Liquor from "pumpkins and parsnips and walnut tree chips" is surely an abominable folk recipe (I cannot find it anywhere). Thoreau was so taken by it that he made it a touchstone for the idea of a New Englander's making-do with the local produce. And although beer can be made from corn, one authority considers it the least desirable method: "There was not sufficient barley mash produced, however, to slake the thirst of the entire colony, so they learned to derive a passable beer malt from oats, rye, old wheat, and even corn." Robert Child mentions beer made from corn in his agricultural tract, *Defects and Remedies of English Husbandry*. When John Winthrop, Jr., wrote a scientific essay on "Indian Corne" for Robert Boyle in 1662, describing, *inter alia*, two ways to make beer from corn—neither method used "green corn stalks." But Robert Beverley, writing in his *History . . . of Virginia* at the opening of the eighteenth century, confirms that "the poorer sort" could brew beer from "the green stalks of Indian corn cut small and bruised." And Peter Kalm, in the mideighteenth century also testified that "the malt of maize tastes exactly like that of barley," although blue corn was considered better than other kinds for malting. (One of the numerous indications that the song dates from the colony's earliest years is the lack of any mention of apple cider—a standard American drink after apple orchards became common in the midseventeenth century.)[19]

Stanza 13 considers one aspect of New England Puritan theology. Among all the possible objections to the New England theology (discussed at length in several publications of the 1630s and 1640s), only the most debatable New England practice is mentioned—the exclusion of a person from church membership if he/she is not judged to have undergone a true conversion experience. Although the Massachusetts churches at first admitted everyone to membership who applied except those known to be of infamous character, by 1636 most churches required that an applicant give a public confession before the congregation of his or her steps to saving grace.[20] Lechford, in *Plain Dealing*, condemned the Massachusetts churches for attempting to "keep out those that have not true grace and what measure God requireth?" He objected to the requirement that the applicants for church membership must narrate their religious experiences "in a solemn speech." Lechford protested that a religious test leads to "Severing in the family." Just as the song condemned the "division 'twixt brother and brother," so Lechford complains "Sometimes the Master is admitted, and not the servant, *& e contra*: the husband is received, and not the wife; and on the contrary, the child, and not the parent."[21] Even some good New England Puritans evidently had reservations about the test as a precondition for church membership. Winthrop recorded in 1644 that "most of those who were to join" the new churches at

Haverhill and Andover "refused to declare how God had carried on the work of his grace in them, upon this reason, because they had declared it formerly in their admission into other churches; whereupon the assembly broke up without proceeding." Since the author of "New England's Annoyances" mentions only this frequently criticized tenet of New England Puritanism, since the tone is reportorial, and since the author does not censure this practice—we may conclude that the author was a New England Puritan who did not himself find the "division" objectionable and who did not think that his main audience would. Therefore the author must have been a New England Puritan writing for New England Puritans. The stanza could not have been written in the early 1630s and probably dates from the early 1640s, when the requirement of a spiritual testimony for church membership was hotly debated.[22] It reinforces the dating suggested by stanzas 6, 7, and 8.

Stanzas 14 and 15 deal with the malcontents who leave New England. The author condemns them on four counts. They are precipitant, finding "fault with our apples before they are mellow." Thus he implies that conditions in New England are improving. The song's criticism was generally valid, especially for those persons who had come over in 1630 and immediately returned.[23] Second, the author says that the alternatives are as bad or worse, because the emigrants "meet with a lion in shunning a bear." Here he echoes Amos 5:19, "As if a man did flee from a lion, and a bear met him," and perhaps glances at 1 Peter 5:8 "because your adversary the devil, as a roaring lion, walketh about, seeking whom he may devour." Of course the bear identification with wilderness New England was a natural one, but the lion is primarily metaphorical. Robert Cushman, in *Mourt's Relation* (1622), used the lion metaphor as a bugbear when he said that objections to the sea voyage to New England and to the danger from pirates or Indians were "but Lyons in the way." Despite the religious and generalized allegorical meaning of "meet with a lion in shunning a bear," I suspect that the author had in mind a specific event—and that the New England audience in the 1640s applied the allusion to a failed remigration attempt. In May 1641, a group of New Englanders, encouraged by Lord Say and Sele and John Humfrey, sailed from Boston for Old Providence (now Santa Catalina) in the West Indies, intending to settle there. But by the time the New Englanders arrived, Spain had taken the island and the Spanish fired on the two Massachusetts boats, killing Captain William Peirce and Samuel

Wakeman. The following September 3, the would-be emigrants arrived back in Massachusetts, chastened and impoverished.[24] They had indeed met with a lion in shunning a bear.

Third, the author condemns those who remigrate as the scum of the colony, "For while liquor is boiling it must have a scumming." And fourth, the song censures them for having naturally dissatisfied dispositions, since "birds of a feather, / By seeking their fellows are flocking together." Taken together, these criticisms of the malcontents tend to date the poem from the early 1640s. John Winthrop repeatedly expresses these attitudes during that period. Winthrop explained in his journal the reasons for the population's decline:

> The sudden fall of land and cattle, and the scarcity of foreign com-modities, and money, etc., with the thin access of people from En-gland, put many into an unsettled frame of spirit, so as they concluded there would be no subsisting here, and according they began to hasten away, some to the West Indies, others to the Dutch, at Long Island, etc., (for the governour there invited them by fair offers,) and others back for England. Among others who returned thither, there was one of the magistrates, Mr. Humfrey, and four ministers, and a schoolmas-ter. These would go against all advice.

Later in the decade, when it was clear that remigration would not ruin New England, Winthrop and other leaders were no longer shocked by the decision to abandon the colony. Thus, in 1645, Winthrop impartially commented that "three honest young men, good scholars, and very hopeful" were leaving. Nor was Edward Johnson upset in 1651 when he told of the brain drain from New England.[25]

The final stanza invites prospective emigrants to come to New England, tells them "Forsake not the honey for fear of the sting," and reassures them they they will find "all needful blessings" in New England if they bring "both a quiet and contented mind." The Reverend John Eliot made the same point when he wrote to Sir Simonds D'Ewes on 18 September 1633. Although Eliot con-demned New England's "heat and cold," he reassured Sir Simonds that the climate was "comfortably tolerable by the weakest, haveing warm houses" and concluded his characterization of Massachusetts with "In a word, I know nothing but is comfortable to a contented mind." And William Wood in his promotion tract used a different application of the "honey . . . sting" metaphor when he discussed the "objections . . . daily invented to hinder the proceedings to these new plantations." He reassured the prospective emigrants that Spain would not raid New England: the English plantations were now "not worth the pillage"; and when they became rich, the Spanish would not raid them, for "when the Bees have Honie in their Hives, they will have stings in their tailes."[26]

The internal historical evidence strongly suggests "New England's Annoyances" was indeed composed *"by one of our first* New-England Planters, *on their Management in those* good *Old Times."* Further, the evidence strongly suggests that it was originally written in the early 1640s. But the date can be determined with precision since a promotion tract of 1643, *New Englands First Fruits*, contains a section that I believe is the primary source for "New England's Annoyances." The pamphlet has been best known as a progress report on Harvard College and as the first of the Eliot Indian tracts. But John Eliot did not write the pamphlet. It was primarily composed by Henry Dunster and Thomas Weld. Dunster evidently wrote the accounts of Harvard and the Indians, and Weld probably wrote the general promotion account (pp. 20–26) dealing with "Divers other speciall Matters concerning that Country." Hugh Peter may have contributed to, or revised, the whole.[27] The eight "objections" that are answered in the pamphlet's conclusion (pp. 24–26) have contents and even a sequence similar to "New England's Annoyances."

The first of eight objections in *New Englands First Fruits*, that "Your ground is barren,"[28] has a counterpart in the song's first annoyance, the complaint of New England's being a "wilderness wood" where the grass was not "fruitful and good" (l. 4). The second objection in *New Englands First Fruits*, "Your ground will not continue above 3 or 4 yeares to beare corne," has no close relationship to any stanza in the song, although stanzas 4 and 5 on the difficulty of raising corn have a similar subject. The third objection is "you have no money there," and the answer maintains "We can trade amongst our selves by way of exchange, one commodity for another, and so doe usually." This complaint is echoed in stanza 6 of "New England's Annoyances": "Our money's soon counted for we have just none, / All that we brought with us is wasted and gone. / We buy and sell nothing but upon exchange, / Which makes all our dealings uncertain and strange." The following objection in *First Fruits* is "You are like to want clothes hereafter," and lack of clothes is also the subject of the song's stanzas 7 and 8. The promotion tract's fifth objection claims that "Your Winters are cold," and the reply grants it—"True, at sometimes when the wind blowes strong at *Nor-West*." The subject of stanzas 2 and 3 in "New England's Annoyances" is the New England cold, particularly the severe "north-wester." The sixth objection, "Many are growne weaker in their estates since they went over," has no counterpart in the song. The pamphlet's final two objections—"Many speake evill of the place" and "Why doe many come away from thence"—both appear in the last three stanzas of "New England's Annoyances." And, like the song, *New Englands First Fruits* concludes on a positive note: "thousands . . . [of New Englanders] would not change their place for any other in the World." The song's topics and sequence are strikingly similar to the pamphlet.

Three topics in the song are absent from the eight objections in *New Englands First Fruits:* the scarcity of English foods—and their replacement by such American ones as pumpkins (stanzas 9 and 10); the lack of beer, and its replacement by American substitutes, especially water (stanzas 11 and 12); and the stanza on the "test" requirement for admission to church membership (stanza 13). But New England's religion is the primary "remarkable passage" of God's providence celebrated in the penultimate section of the pamphlet (pp. 20–23), although Thomas Weld does not specifically mention the test requirement. And the subject of New England's food (stanzas 9 and 10) occurs among the "remarkable" passages of God's providence:

> 7. In giving such plenty of all manner of Food in a Wildernesse insomuch, that all kinds of Flesh, amongst the rest, store of Venison in its season. Fish, both from Sea and Fresh water. Fowle of all kinds, wild and tame; store of Whitemeate, together with all sorts of English Graine, as well as Indian, are plentifull amongst us; as also Rootes, Herbs and Fruit, which being better digested by the Sun, are farre more faire pleasant and wholsome then here.

I also think it significant that three of the commonest complaints about New England are absent from both the song and the pamphlet. First, neither mentions the wolves, although Wood calls them the "greatest inconveniency the Country hath." William Bradford, John White, Edward Winslow, John Winthrop, and Thomas Morton are among the New Englanders who report the annoyance.[29] Second, they both fail to mention snakes—especially rattlesnakes—which were also troublesome. John White, Francis Higginson, Captain John Smith, William Wood, and Thomas Morton all talk of this "most poisonous and dangerous creature, yet nothing so bad as the report goes of him in England" (Wood).

Morton reassures his readers that a rattlesnake "is no lesse hurtful than the adder of England, nor no more." He therefore says that "it is simplicity in any one that shall tell a bugbeare tale of horrible, or terrible Serpents, that are in that land."[30] And third, both the song and the pamphlet omit mosquitoes, which repeatedly turn up as a prime annoyance in the promotion literature. Christopher Levett (1628), John White (1630), and Francis Higginson (1630), among others, mention the mosquito. Bradford, writing in 1624, used the complaint as the occasion for a humorous touch. Answering the objection "The people are much annoyed with mosquitoes," Bradford wrote: "They are too delicate and unfit to begin new plantations and colonies, that cannot endure the biting of a mosquito. We would wish such to keep at home till at least they be mosquito-proof." And Wood, celebrating the advantages of Boston, claims that its inhabitants "are not troubled with three great annoyances, of Woolves, Rattle-snakes, and Musketoes."[31]

Although wolves, rattlesnakes, and mosquitoes, the most common New England "discommodities," are lacking in both pamphlet and song, and although nearly all the subjects—and even something of the sequence—are found in both the pamphlet and the song, it nevertheless may be argued that no relationship existed between the two. The similarities may be attributed to the *zeitgeist*—to the fact that both pamphlet and song reflect the New England conditions of *circa* 1643. And perhaps the similar sequences in the two may be attributable to chance and to the desire of the authors of the song and the pamphlet to conclude on a positive note. . . . Perhaps, but I doubt it. New England was a small society in the 1640s. Every literate New Englander interested in the colony's welfare must have known *New Englands First Fruits* within months of its London publication. And if the song "New England's Annoyances" existed before the pamphlet was written, Thomas Weld must have known it. Common sense dictates that one influenced the other.

Which came first, the song or the pamphlet? The structure of the song is more logical and sequential than *New Englands First Fruits* and especially more so than the "objections answered" conclusion of the pamphlet. Only a complete literary bumbler would change the song's sequence into the pamphlet's rambling order. I therefore think that "New England's Annoyances" was inspired by *New Englands First Fruits.* That means it was composed in 1643, while the same conditions that impelled the composition of *First Fruits* existed and while the pamphlet was fresh in New Englanders' minds.

3
The Earliest American Identities

When did Americans begin to have definite ideas about their difference from Englishmen? Perry Miller thought that John Winthrop and the Massachusetts Bay Puritans were immediately distinguished from their English contemporaries by their sense of a special mission in New England. But Robert Middlekauff claimed that "the founders had no conception of New England apart from Old England" and that such designations (common in the second generation) as a "true New England man" would have been meaningless in the first generation. Although Conrad Cherry granted that Middlekauff was probably right "in claiming that the word 'errand' was not used by the first generation to describe their intentions," he argued that the first colonists did not simply view themselves "as exiles." And Sacvan Bercovitch, without addressing the particular question of the founders' self-identity, stated that the "'process of Americanization' began in Massachusetts not with the decline of Puritanism but with the Great Migration" of 1630.[1] I find abundant evidence in the writings of William Bradford, Edward Winslow, John Winthrop, John Cotton, Thomas Shepard, Thomas Hooker, and Edward Johnson that the founders did, indeed, view themselves as creators of a new civilization, that they fashioned a distinct identity for themselves as "right New England men," and that they soon came to love the place itself, New England, as well as its unique foods and characteristic lifestyle. They took pride in it and in their enormous accomplishment.[2] The most dramatic evidence of early American identity exists in the song that New Englanders popularly adopted and kept alive in the oral tradition.

The song begins by directly addressing "you that would know" New England's annoyances (l. 1) and concludes by directly addressing "you who the Lord intends hither to bring" (l. 61). Therefore it obviously (as all previous accounts of the song testify) is a promotion song, addressed to possible English emigrants. But is it really? Or is the ostensible audience a clever rhetorical strategy? In fact, New Englanders are the real audience. The diction proves it. To Englishmen, especially in the seventeenth century, the word *corn* meant the seed of a cereal (cf. *OED*, s.v. "corn," 2), particularly wheat, rye, or barley. Only in America did *corn* mean "maize" or "Indian corn" (*OED*, s.v. "corn," 5). The reference to "the blade" (l. 18), to "full corn in the ear" (l. 19), and to the "green corn-stalks" (l. 45—this Americanism antedates the earliest recorded usage by nearly 150 years) would only puzzle an English audience. And the native American animal *racoon* (l. 20) would also baffle seventeenth- and eighteenth-century Englishmen.[3] The other specialized diction is religious and narrows the audience from Americans to New Englanders (as, of course, the title and subject suggest). Although the word *covenant* (l. 49) was common in the seventeenth century (it appears seven times in Shakespeare and more than seventy-nine times in the King James Bible), its particular meaning in the song shows that New Englanders were the audience. The system of church membership described in stanza 13 was unique to New England. Thus the "division" (l. 50) refers to the spiritual relation as a test of the beginnings of the work of true grace. All New Englanders understood the reference—but few other people did, except the English puritan theologians who wrote in horror against the New England practice.[4] Further, the usage of "Saints" (*OED*, B. 3—a member of the church by covenant) also suggests that the writer and his audience were Puritans. All *OED* examples of this usage are satirical. Surely not all seventeenth-century, non-Puritan references to this special denotation of *Saints* were satirical—but they certainly tended to be. If the author of "New England's Annoyances" was not a Puritan, he could hardly have written about the "covenant" and the "saints" without satirizing them. The song's diction alone makes it evident that the author must have been a New England Puritan writing for New England Puritans.

Why, then, the rhetorical pretense that the song is addressed to prospective emigrants? The obvious reason is that the song is absurd as promotion propaganda, and so the "inside" audience of New Englanders appreciated the song as a joke. But the underlying reason for pretending to address Englishmen was that it makes the real message of the song acceptable to the poverty-ridden, failing New Englanders of 1643. Many gave up and remigrated to England or to a Southern location, Virginia or the West Indies. Others were thinking of doing so, and all were concerned about the economic situation of New England and the loss of population.[5] But the New

Englanders did not want to be told that leaving New England was traitorous and the devil's work. They knew the difficulties of New England life and certainly did not want to hear promotional propaganda about the fruitful soil, abundance of fish and fowl, or the plentiful increase of Indian corn. On the other hand, the song's portrait of the difficulties of New England life is grossly exaggerated. New Englanders knew that the hardships were not so bad and that the "sting" (l. 62) of the current economic depression could be survived. But they did not want to be told so. And so the songwriter pretends that his song is addressed to prospective emigrants. The speaker in the song is the combined body of New Englanders. "The place where *we* live" (l. 3); "*Our* mountains and hills" (l. 7)— the first-person plural "we" and its possessive "our" is used throughout the song (with two interesting exceptions). The result is the first full self-portrait of the New Englander. And while the self-portrait of the speaker is being made, the real audience (the New Englanders) is being drawn into the song. Thus, by the end of "New England's Annoyances," the audience finds that it is making the pitch to "you who the Lord intends hither to bring" (l. 61). And although the poet does not say so, the pitch applies even more directly to the real audience, people whom the Lord has already brought over. All they need is a "quiet and contented mind" to enjoy "all" the "needful blessings" (l. 64) that New England possesses.

A major subject of "New England's Annoyances" is the characterization of the New Englanders who are its personae. True to its underlying nationalistic spirit, the poem begins with the physical place; for, as Wallace Stevens said, *place* is the most important ingredient of nationalism. New Englanders live in a "wilderness wood" (l. 3) of "mountains and hills and vallies" (l. 7). The image of New England as a remote backwoods, a kind of early American Dogpatch, sets the stage for the foolish hardscrabble hicks who will inhabit it. The cold weather stanzas (2 and 3) tell us that when a "north-wester with violence blows, / Then every man pulls his cap over his nose" (ll. 9–10). The image summoned up of the blinded fool with his cap over his eyes and nose is ridiculous. The author invites the fictive audience of Englishmen to laugh at the blinded New England fool. But the following lines undercut anyone so naive as not to protect himself from the coldest New England weather. Such a condescending person becomes himself the greenhorn who "forfeits a finger, a foot, or a hand" (l. 12).[6] Thus this change of person, from the pervading "we" and "our" to the "any" and "He" (ll. 11–12), employs a rhetorical strategy to undercut the possible critic while at the same time defining New Englanders as old hands who have learned to cope with the elements.

One notes too that, for the first time, an underlying serious, even grim, voice breaks through the burlesque, wry humor that characterizes most of the song. The winters can be deadly and survival is a serious subject. Nevertheless, even these lines have a humorous and patriotic element. Exaggerating hardships is a form of patriotic identification. The Pennsylvanian who bragged in 1744 to Annapolis's Dr. Alexander Hamilton that Pennsylvania's roads were superior to Maryland's because they had more rocks and the "Big B'ar" of Arkansas who boasted of the size and ferocity and usefulness of the Arkansas mosquitoes indulged in similar semi-patriotic ironies.[7]

Stanzas 4 and 5 characterize Americans as backwoods bumpkins who use hoes (up-to-date seventeenth-century farmers had plows) and constantly struggle against the worms, birds, squirrels, hogs, racoons, and deer. In actuality, much if not most New England farming was already done in settled New England communities where fences around the crops limited depredations by hogs and by deer. But the author is again writing not only for his New England audience and for its ideas about its own self-identity, but also for the fictive English audience—and New Englanders' consciousness of what Englishmen generally thought of Americans. Further, although the author mentions "seed being sown" (l. 15), the emphasis is not on the staple English crops (wheat, barley, rye, and oats) that of course were also the common products of American agriculture, but upon the distinctive American crop, Indian corn. This patriotic note appeals to the distinguishing foods and communal experiences of Americans. To this point in the poem, the author's deliberate caricature has defined New Englanders as foolish, backward, backwoods, hardscrabble corn-growers.

Stanza 6, on currency, adds to the portrait of New Englanders as impoverished rustics who "buy and sell nothing but upon exchange, / Which makes all our dealings uncertain and strange." The following two stanzas reveal that they have no wool "to card and to spin" (l. 26) and that their clothes are all torn and patched, and patched upon patch. This caricature of the backwoods farmer's clothing matches that of the comic-strip Snuffy Smith. It is obviously a grotesque exaggeration—but once again the author himself reveals that he identifies with the portrait and expects his audience not to scorn the figure, "For clouting our garments does injure us nothing: / Clouts double are warmer than single whole clothing" (ll. 31–32).

Stanzas 9 and 10 portray Americans as necessitous rustics who lack "flesh meat" but usually have "carrots and pumpkins and turnips and fish." Turnips in this stanza and parsnips in the next stress the poorest possibilities of standard English foods. Indeed, the opening of stanza 13 contrasts and grossly exaggerates the difference between the diet of English and American farmers: "Instead of pottage and puddings and custards and pies, / Our pumpkins and parsnips are common supplies." The English all supposedly enjoy middle-class foods, while the Americans barely manage to subsist. In fact, by 1643, New England annually had a great surplus of food. Like the other historical sources, Edward Johnson testified that "flesh is now no rare food, beef, pork, and mutton being frequent in many houses, so that this poor Wilderness hath not only equalized England in food, but goes beyond it in some places for the great plenty of wine and sugar which is ordinarily spent, apples, pears, and quince tarts instead of their former Pumpkin Pies."[8] By fusing the entirely different starving times of the 1620s and 1630s with the economic depression of the 1640s, the author of "New England's Annoyances" creates a mythic New England age of hardship and poverty. Of course it makes his portrait of New Englanders as hardscrabble hicks more dramatic but, more important, it emphasizes the past trials and thus the achievements of New Englanders in conquering these difficulties.

Stanzas 11 and 12 further develop the portrait of New Englanders as hillbillies. Here the New Englanders anticipate that favorite Southern folk hero, the moonshiner, but instead of using corn, the New Englanders brew an incredible concoction "Of pumpkins and parsnips and walnut tree chips" (l. 44). This, I submit, is the fictive world of Hairless Joe, Lonesome Pine, and Kickapoo Joy Juice.[9] The beer was almost as outlandish as the liquor. Although most New England beer was brewed in the standard manner, from barley, beer can be made from various vegetables and corn; and although there are two usual ways to make acceptable beer from corn, these hardscrabble New England rustics make their "best beer" (l. 45) in the worst possible way—from "green cornstalks" (l. 45). In stanza 12's last couplet, the author uses the first person singular for the first and only time in the song when he reveals that he himself is not among the hard-drinking hillbillies described in the last six lines: "Yet I am as healthy, I verily think, / Who make the spring water my commonest drink." This sober—

even ascetic note—marks the song's turn away from the portrait of the New Englanders as Snuffy Smiths—backwoods bumpkins dressed in ragged, patched, and repatched old clothes who pull their caps down over their noses in the winter, hoe their corn in the spring, eat their pumpkins at morning and noon, and drink their own strange moonshine throughout the year. That self-caricature was the first identity that New Englanders popularly adopted.

At the end of stanza 12, the subject matter changes. The mock portrait of the New Englanders and the list of the supposed "Annoyances" is complete. Suitably, these changes in subject, personae and tone lead into stanza 13, devoted to New England's religion. The author states that their "Cov'nant . . . makes a division 'twixt brother and brother" (l. 50). No exaggeration, no burlesque personae, and no humor exist in this stanza, for the author and his audience believe God rejects some and selects others. Man cannot change that. The theological system designed by the New England Puritans attempted to copy the judgment of the Puritan God. They knew it must be an imperfect copy, but they knew that God made divisions " 'twixt brother and brother." Indeed, the author departs from the actual New England theology in stanza 13, for the church did not discriminate between those who really appeared to be "equal in Virtues and Wants." Both brothers, if they gave satisfying spiritual relations and were known to be reasonably well-behaved, would be admitted. Neither brother, of course, would in the Puritan theology *deserve* to be saved, and the Puritan God would indeed make "a division" between those who appeared to be "equal in Virtues and Wants." In this stanza the song does not describe the literal reality but repeats a common slander on the New England Way in order to assert a theological truth—and what better defense could a good New England Puritan make to an audience of New England Puritans?

The opening of stanza 14 tells the audience that the catalogue of "annoyances" is over. The concluding three stanzas deal with the remigration from New England and with the emigration to New England. The final stanza ends on a strong religious note. Proverbs and sententiae characterize stanzas 14 through 16. Although only two brief commonplaces occur in the first thirteen stanzas ("hard as a stone," 6; "clout upon clout," 28), fully half of the lines in the last three quatrains are proverbial expressions, sententiae, or clichés: "find fault with our apples before they are mellow"; "meet with a lion in shunning a bear"; "while liquor is boiling it must have a scumming"; "birds of a feather . . . are flocking together"; "Forsake not the honey for fear of a sting"; and "a quiet and contented mind" providing "all needful blessings." The rhetorical effect of all these commonplaces is to make the argument seem natural, even indisputable. Who would contradict the commonsense observations and proverbial wisdom that constitute the concluding stanzas?

The religious references in these quatrains reinforce the rhetorical strategy and follow naturally after stanza 13. The biblical allusion to the "mad fellows" (l. 53) who return to England and "meet with a lion in shunning a bear" (alluding to Amos 5:19) compares New England's malcontents to the "wicked and hypocrites" who foolishly hope to escape God's judgments.[10] The speaker says that such "mad fellows" will be unhappy anywhere, and he implies that their decision to leave New England indicates their rejection of God and thus signifies their eternal damnation. The penultimate stanza indirectly calls them "scum" and condemns them to similar company ("birds of a feather") here and hereafter. The only direct reference to God occurs in the final stanza. In the song's rhetorically most important place, the poet drops the active for the passive voice. The change from active to passive might normally be a blemish, deadening the action. But the author knew what he was doing. He indirectly reminds his audience that God is really all-powerful and that man is actually passive and dependent. The metaphysics shared by all Christians thus reinforces and confirms the poet's message. Who can deny the fundamental truth of the poet's conclusion when the action is really God's? The poet addresses "you who the Lord intends hither to bring." But of course the New Englanders who the poet is really addressing are those whom God has already brought over. The author reaffirms that difficulties exist ("Forsake not the honey for fear of the sting") but claims they are minor in comparison to the rewards—which, he implies, are true grace and eternal salvation. The one requirement in order to find true happiness in New England is "a quiet and contented mind" (l. 63), a phrase that recalls and contrasts with the "mad fellows" (l. 53) who leave New England. And the religious connotations of "blessings" in the last line reaffirm the spiritual message of the final four stanzas, while the modifying "needful" recalls the "annoyances" catalogued throughout the song.

"New England's Annoyances" is an American product because of its subject matter (especially the native plants), genre, persona, rhetorical postures, patriotism, and underlying ideology. It is the earliest example of a characteristically American literary genre—a piece that mocks both the promotion literature and the satires on the promotion literature. Perhaps the best-known colonial example is Ebenezer Cook's *Sot-Weed Factor* (1708), which ostensibly satirizes the frontier conditions of, as the long title says, *the laws, government, courts and constitutions of the country; and also the buildings, feasts, frolics, entertainment and drunken humors of the inhabitants of that part of America.* But, for the "knowing American," Cook actually lampoons the foolish preconceptions of the supposedly sophisticated English persona who is really both a greenhorn and a fool. Cook mocks the speaker's fears of Indians, rattlesnakes, and wolves, and the typical English perception of Americans as barbarians. Like all colonial Americans interested in literature, Cook thoroughly knew the traditions both of promotion literature and the anti-American satires; and so he, like the author of "New England's Annoyances," pretended to write for an English audience while really addressing his work to fellow Americans.[11]

Promotion literature, satires on the promotion literature, and replies to the satires together constitute a major tradition in American literature and a dominant tradition in American humor. Anonymous brief colonial satires and works by the most important colonial authors (including William Byrd, Dr. Alexander Hamilton, and Benjamin Franklin) use the tradition. Nor did it end in the eighteenth century. As new territories opened throughout the nineteenth century and as promoters prepared new developments in the twentieth century, promotional propaganda appeared, followed by satires and replies to the satires. From Sir Walter Ralegh's colony to the Georgia colony, from the Louisiana Purchase to Seward's Folly, from the sodbuster's frontier to a recent real estate development in Needles, California, the motifs are similar.[12] One popular nineteenth-century American folk song, said to embody the American pioneer spirit, uses the same ironic boasting that characterizes "New England's Annoyances." "The Lane County Bachelor" begins: "Hurrah for Lane County, the land of the free, / The home of the grasshopper, bedbug and flea; / I'll sing loud its praises and tell of its fame, / While starving to death on my government claim." Other antipromotion folksongs employing similar ironic boasting include "Little Old Sod Shanty on the Plain," "Sanford Barney," and "Sweet Nebraskaland." Norwegian and Swedish emigrants' songs burlesque the promise of American abundance by portraying America as lubberland.[13] In what is reputedly the funniest speech ever delivered in Congress, James Proctor Knott, on 27 January 1871, burlesqued the promotional literature celebrating Duluth, Minnesota. The classic story in the humor of the Old

South, T. B. Thorpe's "The Big Bear of Arkansas," spoofed the promotional traditions. And Mark Twain, America's greatest humorist, repeatedly used the motifs and techniques of promotion, antipromotion, and the replies to the antipromotion literature.[14] "New England's Annoyances" inaugurates an important tradition in American humor and American literature. Its humor and satire must have had a major impact—comparable to, say, "The Little Old Sod Shanty on the Plain" when everyone knew W. S. Hayes's song "The Little Old Log Cabin in the Lane." Just as Ebenezer Cook structured his *Sot-Weed Factor* upon the popular antipromotion song "A West Country Man's Voyage to New England," so the author of "New England's Annoyances" followed the organization of the usual promotion tract. The place, climate, crops, and drink are the consecutive subjects in "New England's Annoyances" and in nearly all promotion tracts—which generally conclude with an appeal for emigrants and often with a final list of tools and supplies useful in a new plantation. The song omits the supplies but tells the emigrant to bring "a quiet and contented mind."[15]

The song also burlesques the antipromotion literature. Dwelling upon and exaggerating New England's hardships mocks the satires. But at the same time, the author reminds New Englanders of their past heroic efforts and makes them want to persevere. He uses various appeals to New Englanders' patriotic feelings—dwelling upon the place itself, upon America's unique foods and folkways, and upon a mock portrait of the "character" of an American. Corn and pumpkins make their earliest deliberate literary appearances as symbols of American identity in "New England's Annoyances." Everyone knows of Plymouth Colony's early dependence on corn and here is John Winthrop's Massachusetts Bay tribute to corn, written to his wife, 29 November 1630: "we are heer in Paradice, though we have not beife and mutton etc: yet (God be praysed) we want them not; our Indian Corne answeares for all." Winthrop's comment indicates his incipient acculturation; for, as Stephen Vincent Benét claimed, corn-eating symbolized Americanization:

> And those who came were resolved to be Englishmen,
> Gone to the world's end, but English every one,
> And they ate the white corn-kernels, parched in the sun,
> And they knew it not, but they'd not be English again.[16]

The use of corn in "New England's Annoyances" anticipates its appearance in such eighteenth-century nationalistic (and some anti-

American) works as "Yankee Doodle" (the "Corn Stalks" stanzas), Benjamin Franklin's essay signed "Homespun," Jonathan Boucher's "Absence, a Pastoral," Joel Barlow's "Hasty Pudding," and *The Adventures of Jonathan Corncob*.[17] All these eighteenth-century works proclaim the distinctive Americanness of corn—and, like "New England's Annoyances," characterize Americans as corn-eaters.

In attempting to create an American identity, the author also celebrates pumpkins as a distinctive American food: "We have pumpkin at morning and pumpkin at noon, / If it was not for pumpkins we would be undone" (ll. 39–40). The tradition of pumpkin pie at Thanksgiving attests to the American—and New England—identity of pumpkins. I believe the poet Benjamin Tompson, writing a generation later, had these lines from "New England's Annoyances" in mind when he opened "The Prologue" to *New England's Crisis* (1676) with "The times wherein old *Pompion* was a Saint, / When men far'd hardly yet without complaint / On vilest Cates." So far as I know, the earliest writer to make use of corn and pumpkins in order to create and celebrate a distinctive American identity was the author of "New England's Annoyances." Identifying corn and pumpkins as the lifestay of the early settlers was true—but it was also myth, making the starving-time beginnings of the puritan errand a particularly American experience. The foods came to symbolize the communal spirit of achievement associated with both the difficult beginnings and the ultimate success of American colonization.[18] "New England's Annoyances" is still too close to the actual experience of starvation to label those days the "golden times" or "our most happy times"—that perspective took another generation. (As Franklin wrote, "The Golden Age never was the present age.")[19] But the song began the myth: the early starving time was an ideal age when all the colonists supposedly experienced the same hardships and communally strived to achieve the same goals. The song uses these ordeals to remind New Englanders of their accomplishments, the settlement of New England, and the creation of a new state. Recalling the hardships and starving times patriotically asserts New England's material and nationalistic success. The founders agreed: they had suffered extraordinary hardships but had created a new civilization. When the immigration ceased in 1640, Winthrop referred sarcastically to English expectations of "a new world." *He* knew that New England was the New World. Edward Johnson wrote that New England "is the place where the Lord will create a new Heaven, and a New

Earth in, new churches, and a new Common–wealth together." He called the colonists' achievement in creating this new civilization "indeed the wonder of the world."[20] The song's emotional appeal to the New England Puritan anticipates, in part, that characteristic New England sermon of the late seventeenth century, the Jeremiad. "New England's Annoyances" implicitly points out that New Englanders are falling away from their earlier ideals and recalls them to the faith. As it does so, the song welds New Englanders together.

The author's most brilliant stroke is his portrait of the New Englander as a hardscrabbler. Two major identities for Americans had already been well established, the planter-farmer and the rustic-hick. The earliest name for an American was a *planter*. The Virginia literature repeatedly calls the actual settlers in America *planters*, i.e., those who go out to found a colony (*OED* 3; *DAE* 1). The first planters were as celebrated, in the different circumstances of their own day, as the earliest astronauts are in this time. Captain John Smith's *Map of Virginia* (1612) features a list of the names of the "first planters." And the dedication says: "to speake truly of the first planters, that brake the yce and beate the path, howsoever many difficulties obscured their indevours, he were worse then the worst of Ingrates, that would not spare them memory that have buried themselves in those forrain regions. From whose first adventures may spring more good blessings than are yet conceived."[21] And the very title of Captain John Smith's most ambitious work emphasizes the fame of the earliest Americans—*The General History of Virginia, New-England and the Summer Isles: with the names of the Adventurers, Planters, and Governours from their first beginning. Anno. 1584. to this present 1624.* When the Pilgrim Fathers sailed in 1620 and when Winthrop's great fleet sailed in 1630, the voyagers already knew their future identity: they would be, as John Winthrop wrote the year before he sailed, the "first planters" of their Massachusetts Bay Colony. Although John Smith once referred bitterly to so many "first planters" (thinking, with some justice, that the Virginians in 1607 were the real "first planters"), he elsewhere approvingly labeled the Pilgrim Fathers the "first planters" of Plymouth Colony.[22]

But the idea of American identity was more noble than the actuality. It might seem glorious to explore new lands, to found a new colony and a new civilization, and to become (like Captain John Smith) famous. But the reality was back-breaking, often dangerous, impoverishing work. The older and primary meaning of *planter* as a farmer (*OED* 1) always lurked behind its more glamorous denotation. Although William Bradford, in his history *Of Plymouth Plantation*, primarily uses *planter* to refer to the colonists in general, he occasionally uses it to distinguish the farmers from such other colonists as traders and fishermen (1:447; cf. 1:434 and 2:17). Thus the meaning of *planter* for the earliest colonists was both a founder of a plantation and a farmer. By the time that he wrote the following apology for his prose style, the Puritan theologian Thomas Hooker (1586?–1647), who emigrated to New England in 1633, revealed that he had adopted an American identity: "That the discourse comes forth in such a homely dresse and course habit, the Reader must be desired to consider, It comes *out of the Wilderness*, where curiosity is not studied. Planters if they can provide cloth to go warm, they leave the cutts and lace to those that study to go fine."[23] Even the New England Puritan theologian called Americans "planters" and identified himself with the poor, tough American farmer, barely able to keep warm in the "wilderness" of New England.

That rustic-hick self-image has been synonymous with America from the very first settlers until at least the time of the expatriates after the First World War, for America has constantly been identified with wilderness or remote backwoods, with lack of sophistication, and with provincialism. Even such a cosmopolite as George Sandys, whom Dryden called "the best versifier of the former age," apologized for his translation of Ovid because it was "bred in the New World, the rudenesse whereof it cannot but participate." Writing on 30 September 1619 from Virginia to his patron in England, John Pory said, "at my first coming hither the solitary uncouthness of this place compared with those parts of Christendome or Turkey where I had been; and likewise my being sequestered from all accurrents and passages which are so rife there, did not a little vex me."[24] And Captain John Smith, completing the fourth book devoted to Virginia in his *General History*, thought the metaphor suitable for his conclusion: "Thus far have I travelled in this Wilderness of Virginia." In New England, John Winthrop realized that living in America necessarily involved him—in the eyes of his English contemporaries—in the inexorable process of becoming a rustic, a hick. And so the sophisticated Winthrop in 1646 identifies himself with "such poor rustics as a wilderness can breed up." But, like the Pennsylvania frontiersman Benjamin Sutton in the 1760s or like the wigless Benjamin Franklin in Paris during the American Revolution, John Winthrop used the pose to disarm his supposedly more cosmopolitan contemporaries.[25] The pretense was a trap that would expose the foolishness of the sophisticate—but only, of course, if the sophisticate really believed in his essential superiority. As one of Franklin's "very shrewd" English friends perceived, the combination of a seemingly straightforward persona with a put-on was the characteristic "American" joke.[26] The anti-American satires, rife in England, almost invariably portrayed the emigrant as a fool. English and European condescension was a constant source of gall to Americans. And one typical response was to pretend to be a hick.[27] This persona, splendidly used in America's great eighteenth-century folksong "Yankee Doodle," first appeared in that patch-upon-patch, hoe-swinging, corn-growing, pumpkin-eating hardscrabbler, whose "best beer" was made from green cornstalks and whose moonshine was concocted from "pumpkins and parsnips and walnut-tree chips." New Englanders adopted the caricature and enjoyed the joke. But if the English heard the song, they would not know that it was a put-on. "New England's Annoyances" marks the first appearance of the backwoods yokel as American. This deliberate bamboozlement became a dominant rhetorical strategy for later American literature and culture.

The hardscrabbler of "New England's Annoyances" is the ancestor of that dominant twentieth-century self-image of Americans, the hillbilly. One can trace the lineage back from today's Beverly Hillbillies, Louis L'Amour's Sacketts, Al Capp's "Li'l Abner," Billy De Beck's "Snuffy Smith," and, of course, the poor-whites of William Faulkner and Erskine Caldwell to the humor of the Old South and to James Russell Lowell's *Bigelow Papers* and before them to the colonial period.[28] Thomas Cradock's transported felons, Robert Bolling's disgusting low-lifes, Franklin's rustic personae (e.g., "Homespun"), the yokel persona of "Yankee Doodle," the backwoods barbarians of William Byrd's North Carolina, and the "Indian-like" bumpkins of Sarah Kemble Knight's 1704 journal (who have "as Large a portion of mother witt, and sometimes a Larger, than those who have bin brought up in citties")—these are among the hillbillies' eighteenth-century ancestors.[29] And their progenitor was the seventeenth-century hardscrabbler of "New England's Annoyances."

Part of the appeal of the song was its underlying religious ideology. As the four concluding quatrains make clear, the song reminds New Englanders that their primary purposes were not and are not mere material considerations but God's grace and their own salvation. "New England's Annoyances" burlesques the lubberland motifs of the promotion and antipromotion literature. In *Information to Those Who Would Remove to America* (1782), Benjamin Franklin used a similar strategy when he wrote: "America is the Land of Labour, and by no means what the English call *Lubberland*, and the French *Pays de Cocagne*, where the streets are said to be pav'd with half-peck Loaves, the Houses til'd with Pancakes, and where the Fowls fly about ready roasted, crying *Come eat me!*"[30] But a key difference exists between Franklin's *Information* (and so many other spoofs of the promotional tradition) and "New England's Annoyances," for the song's underlying authorial voice is basically religious. The metaphysical ideology of "New England's Annoyances" finds an apt symbol in the hardscrabbler. The Puritan God did not intend the world to be a garden of sensual delights. William Bradford expresses the proper Puritan spirit memorably: "So theye lefte the goodly and plesante citie, which had been ther resting place near 12 years; but they knew they were pilgrimes, and looked not much on those things, but lift up their eyes to the heavens, their dearest cuntrie, and quieted their spirits."[31] "New England's Annoyances" asserts the same underlying message. And with its ultimate authorial voice, it actually (not just humorously) celebrates the hardships and deprivations because they mirror the Puritan's deepest suspicions of worldly temptations. Again, Bradford is a touchstone. His account of the Pilgrim Fathers' early hardships (written more than twenty-five years later) concludes: "Man lives not by bread only, Deut: 8.3. It is not by good and dainty fare, by peace, and rest, and harts ease, in injoying the contentments and good things of this world only, that preserves health and prolongs life. God in shuch examples would have the world see and behold that he can doe it without them; and if the world will shut ther eyes, and take no notice therof, yet he would have his people to see and consider it."[32]

But no writer's words reveal the basic Puritan suspicions of lubberland so well as John Endecott's symbolic action. His cutting down the maypole at Merrymount epitomizes the Puritan's hostility to the idea of the earthly paradise.[33] Both William Bradford and Nathaniel Hawthorne appreciated the symbolic oppositions underlying that incident. Thomas Morton celebrated abundance and sensuality with the traditional fertility rituals, but the scene violated the Puritans' ascetic spiritual values.[34] "New England's Annoyances" is ultimately a religious song, recalling not only the facts of past material privations but indirectly asserting that those priva-

tions indicate a spiritual superiority. Therefore it seems especially
fitting that the song should be New England's first folk song, and
fitting too that it died out from the American folk tradition in the
late eighteenth century. What remains and triumphs from puritan
times in present folkways are the corn and pumpkin pie at Thanksgiving Day—a feast that hedonistic moderns have foisted on our
forefathers.[35]

But if the religious ideology symbolized by the hardscrabbler is
no longer such an important aspect of American literature and
culture, why does the figure persist in so many later transforma-
tions? The primary reason this persona became—and remains—a
dominant American self-characterization is because it asserts
America's democratic values. The song repeatedly implies the dignity and worth of the ostensible personae who are its subjects. For
example, when the ragged and patched farmers are described, the
song says that if the impoverished planters are lucky enough to
have a coat "to cover without," their underclothing is "clout upon
clout" (l. 28). That phrase recalls the seventeenth-century proverbial saying "Patch by patch is good housewifery, but patch upon
patch is plain beggary."[36] But the strange bragging in the song
undercuts possible condescension as the author realistically asserts
that "clouts double are warmer than single whole clothing" (l. 32).
With this assertion the author deliberately contradicts the traditional beggarly and unworthy connotations of "patch upon patch."
To the English proverb's scorn, the American folksong replies with
a practical argument—and thus indirectly asserts the equality, even
the superiority—of the poor person who wears "clout upon clout."

The portrait of Americans as a group of poor but tough farmers
who take pride in their achievement (which as they well knew was
the founding of a civilization) becomes more important than the
song's underlying religious thesis. The song proclaims the tough
sufficiency of the poor—and makes that tough sufficiency a virtue.
It thus implicitly advocates a radical democracy. Thomas Hooker's
apology for his prose style (quoted above, p. 61) also contains this
democratic belief. It is certainly not Hooker's primary purpose to
dignify "a homely dress and course habit," nor to celebrate the
influence of the American wilderness, nor to say that planters prefer "warm cloth" to "cutts and lace." But the terms of his apology
(and the tone) tend to justify and even praise "a homely dress and
course habit," to extol the influence of the wilderness (a return to
basics is implied), and to prefer a poor planter's "warm cloth" to a
wealthy aristocrat's "cutts and lace." In short, Hooker's metaphors

imply a radical democratic philosophy—even though his basic purpose is certainly a literary apology. The saying of a clergyman in the Revolutionary period testifies that the song's feelings and even something of its language continued in the American tradition. A younger contemporary testified that Devereux Jarratt (1733–1801) often exhorted his "fellow citizens . . . even to go *patch upon patch* rather than suffer their just rights to be infringed."[37]

"New England's Annoyances," America's first folksong, is a significant work in American literature and culture because of its aesthetic embodiment of so many American attitudes. The seventeenth-century American Puritanism that animates it and assures the New Englanders that they should persevere and that they will ultimately succeed is one major ingredient. The natural human attempt to create humor in response to any extended hardship, whether it be a frontier or war experience, is another. The colonial's or rustic's reaction to the assumed superiority of the colonizing country or of the "city-slicker" is a third. The belief in the essential equality of all men and in the fragility of human existence is a fourth ingredient. Although religion became less important as time went on, and although the idea of American cultural inferiority ended with the second world war, traces of these attitudes still exist today. And the American belief in democracy and in the worth and dignity of the individual is as strong or stronger than it ever was. "New England's Annoyances" not only embodied those American attitudes but it also used the rhetorical strategies that were to be so important in promulgating the underlying American ideologies. The primary ingredient of those rhetorical strategies is the creation of a rustic and/or simpleton persona who directly or indirectly satirizes the supercilious condescension of the audience, whether that audience exists within the fictive work or is itself a fiction. And such a fictive audience (standing, of course, for real attitudes) always exists as an important part of the fictive universe of the American put-on. "New England's Annoyances" presents an early full portrait of American identity and, in an analysis, reveals not only the characteristics that constitute that identity but also the reasons why the earliest Americans adopted those characteristics.

4
Who Wrote the Song?

I have argued that "New England's Annoyances" was written *circa* 1643 by a New England Puritan. Since New England was a comparatively small society in the 1640s, since the writers (and especially the poets) of early New England are well known, and since I (like many other students of early American literature) have read most of the extant poetry and much of the prose, it should be possible to make a reasonable guess concerning who wrote the song. Although the author of "New England's Annoyances" may not have written anything else extant, he or she probably was one of New England's known authors.

First, I should dispose of the red herring. In 1880, Justin Winsor attributed "New England's Annoyances" to Benjamin Tompson (1642–1714). Winsor gave no evidence or argument for the attribution. I suspect Winsor made a careless slip, prompted by the association of the subjects of "New England's Annoyances" with the same topics in Tompson's "Prologue" to *New Englands Crisis* (Boston 1676). Indeed, Winsor may even have confused the two poems, although he may be citing "The Prologue" simply as an example of the supposed "privations" of the 1630s. Certainly the speakers' attitudes within the two poems are entirely different. Tompson sentimentalizes the good old days of the 1630s (which he calls the "golden times") and opposes them to the ills of contemporary (1676) society. On the other hand, the author of "New England's Annoyances" wryly exaggerates the hardships while using them as symbols of spiritual truths. Even though "New England's Annoyances" has an element of nostalgia for the hard times of the 1630s, the speaker's primary attitude is that the hard times still threaten. Besides, Tompson was not born until 1642 and so could not have written a poem dating from the 1640s. Winsor wrote:

> His name [Benjamin Tompson] is kept alive by what is usually quoted as 'Our Forefathers' Song,' a bit of verse with a rather lively swing to it, picturing the privations of the earlier times, when

he echoes the song, I do not believe that he wrote it. The author of "New England's Annoyances" combines a certain grimness and undercurrent of spiritual truth in his descriptions of New England's hard times. Though he uses wry humor in his exaggeration, the author has an underlying serious voice. Although Danforth can be, at times, humorous and serious, he lacks the stern quality of voice underlying "New England's Annoyances." And Danforth (b. 1626) seems too young—both as a poet and a person—to have written "New England's Annoyances." The song's author evidently experienced the cold, hoed the fields, lived through the starving time, and helped create the New England theology. Danforth's life testifies that he did not suffer these hardships. Third, the song is more mature—and better—than any of Danforth's surviving verse, all of which was composed at least several years later than 1643. He was not our author.

Edward Johnson (1598–1672) is the logical choice. He is best known for his *History of New England* (London, 1654 [for 1653]), which stresses a millenarian interpretation of New England as the New Jerusalem. Johnson ranks among New England's best writers. Like William Bradford and Edward Winslow, he had little formal education, but his extraordinary abilities were clearly recognized (as were Bradford's and Winslow's) by his contemporaries. The dominant town father of Woburn, Massachusetts, Johnson represented Woburn in the legislature nearly every year, serving as town clerk, captain of the militia, surveyor, selectman, and magistrate. He was the town's indispensable citizen. A leader in the Massachusetts legislature, he served as Speaker *pro tem* in 1655 and was a member of a small committee chosen to protect the colony's charter in 1664.[11] Nor is *The History of New England* his only published book. All scholars who have studied the promotion tract *Good News From New England* (London, 1648) agree that Johnson also wrote it.[12] "New England's Annoyances" contains more similarities in style and tone, content, and underlying mood to Johnson's two works than to any other seventeenth-century New England writing. Further, *Good News From New England* is mainly in verse, and *A History of New England* contains sixty-seven poems.[13] Johnson's humor and literary ability also clearly appear in the town records of Woburn, especially in the fine poem prefacing those records.[14] The best authority on seventeenth-century American poetry, Professor Harold S. Jantz, suggested in 1943 that Johnson wrote "New England's Annoyances." In assessing Johnson's poetry, Professor Jantz included "the so-called 'Our Forefathers' Song,' full of high

America (London, 1647). Ward's style is usually colloquial and homely, and his persona in *The Simple Cobler* combines the naif, the Indian, and the rustic. He was celebrated by his contemporaries and the next generation for his wit and humor. But two reasons make one suspect that Ward did not write "New England's Annoyances." First, he returned to England in 1646, and the spirit underlying the song would have judged him a malcontent. Second, Ward is unable to resist a learned pun, a polysyllabic nonce word, or erudite diction.[9] I do not think he could have written the consistently simple and colloquial couplets of "New England's Annoyances."

Samuel Danforth, who graduated from Harvard in 1642, wrote a series of almanac poems in the 1640s very similar in subject and spirit to "New England's Annoyances." Danforth, who came at age eight to New England in 1634, became a good Puritan and pastor of the Roxbury church. His witty almanac verses may even echo "New England's Annoyances." In the almanac for 1647/8, he writes about the bitter New England winters (the verses for December and January), about the raising of corn (August), about the economy and malcontents (September), and about New England's religion (June).[10] In the almanac for 1648/9, he uses bird imagery like that in "New England's Annoyances" (ll. 59–60) to describe those who returned to England: "Those Birds of prey, who sometime have opprest / And stain'd the Country with their filthy nest." And he portrays the economy and a "contented" mind in a passage that probably echoes the song:

> Few think, who only hear, but doe not see,
> That PLENTY groweth much upon this tree.
> That since the mighty COW her crown hath lost,
> In every place shee's made to rule the rost;
> That heaps of Wheat, Pork, Bisket, Beef & Beer
> Masts, Pipe-staves, Fish should store both farre & neer:
> Which fetch in Wines, Cloth, Sweets & good Tobacc-
> O be contented then, you cannot lack.

(65–72)

The "mighty COW" refers to the disastrous fall in price of cattle in 1640; but the verse paragraph describes the subsequent recovery of New England's economy and its growing trade: "Wheat, Pork . . . Fish" for "Wines, Cloth . . . Tobacc." Despite the fact that Danforth wrote good humorous verse on the same subjects as the author of "New England's Annoyances," and despite the possibility that

New England's Prospect is not a good poet. His brief iambic pentameter couplets are all clumsy. Further, the author of *New England's Prospect* displays no religious feeling and little interest in religion. Alden T. Vaughan has pointed out that "Wood's departure in 1633, combined with the relatively secular tone of his writing, suggests that he may have been a New Englander but not a Puritan."[5] So even if the author of *New England's Prospect* were living in Massachusetts in the 1640s, I think it extremely unlikely that he could or would have written a fundamentally puritan song.

Although Thomas Morton, like Wood, has humorous talent, and although Morton writes interesting poetry, he could not have written "New England's Annoyances." In *New English Canaan* (Amsterdam, 1637), Morton overpraises the climate, fertility, and abundance of New England, ignores the difficulties of colonization, and celebrates the area as Canaan, a paradise of ease and plenty. Morton presents New England as a lubberland. He takes no delight in the difficulties of life nor does he see them as symbols of spiritual reality. He is an Anglican and anti-Puritan.[6] Drop Morton.

Thomas Weld (1595–1660/1), who emigrated to New England in 1632, wrote a number of the psalms in the "Bay Psalm Book" (1640), the last part of *New Englands First Fruits* (London, 1643), and *An Answer to W[illiam] R[atbband]* (London, 1644). He displays an occasional humorous flair, and his translations of psalms prove that he could and did write poetry. But Weld left New England in 1641 and never returned. If "New England's Annoyances" were really a promotion song—i.e., if it were directed to Englishmen rather than to New Englanders—Weld would be a logical possibility as the author. A poet and a Puritan, he had considerable literary ability, employed humor in his writings, and was the primary agent of Massachusetts Bay in England in the 1640s.[7] But the song was written for New England Puritans *circa* 1643 and condemns the malcontents who leave New England. It is extraordinarily unlikely that Weld, in England, would have written it. The same is true for Hugh Peter (1599–1660), who sailed to England with Weld as an agent for Massachusetts Bay in 1641. Although Peter, a noted wit, wrote poetry, he (like Weld) could hardly have written "New England's Annoyances" while living in England in 1643.[8] It would have been rank hypocrisy. Besides, neither Weld nor Peter was, so far as we know, an interesting poet.

Nathaniel Ward (1578–1652) might seem to be a logical choice, for he wrote a good deal of poetry and penned the classic humorous work of puritan New England, *The Simple Cobler of Aggawam in*

"The dainty Indian Maize
Was eat with clam shells out of wooden trays,
Under thatched hutts without the cry of rent,
And the best sauce to every dish, Content."[1]

Tompson does indeed seem to echo "New England's Annoyances" in "The Prologue" to *New England's Crisis* (1676)—just as he echoes Edward Johnson's *History of New England* (London, 1654) and Nathaniel Ward's *Simple Cobler of Aggawam* (London, 1644) in his poem "To Lord Bellamont" (1699)[2]—but I can not believe that he wrote the song.

The best first-generation poet was Anne Bradstreet, but she primarily wrote for a circle of patrician peers. The hillbilly hero/narrator of "New England's Annoyances," swilling his home brew of pumpkins and parsnips and walnut-tree chips, is simply not within her repertoire of styles or feelings. Although Roger Williams emigrated to Massachusetts in 1630 and had considerable poetic ability, he was banished from the Bay Colony in 1636. Besides, he did not believe in the necessity for a spiritual relation as a condition for church membership. The underlying Puritanism of "New England's Annoyances" was, by 1643, antithetic to Williams. Indeed, by that date, Rhode Island and Massachusetts were on the brink of war, and so he would not then have encouraged emigration to Massachusetts. Williams, like Anne Bradstreet, may easily be ruled out.

Of the well-known New England authors who flourished between 1635 and 1655, only William Wood, Thomas Morton, Thomas Weld, Hugh Peter, Nathaniel Ward, Samuel Danforth, and Edward Johnson frequently reveal the burlesque and humorous traits that characterize "New England's Annoyances," I shall briefly examine the possibility that one of them wrote the song. From his humor and from his use of an occasional phrase that also turns up in the song, Wood, author of *New England's Prospect*, might seem to be a likely candidate. But nothing is positively known about Wood after the publication of his promotion tract. He may have died soon thereafter, he may never have returned to America, or he may be the same William Wood who emigrated to America in 1635 and settled in Lynn, Massachusetts.[3] Since no literary associations with any William Wood exist after 1634, I doubt that the talented author of *New England's Prospect* actually returned to America.[4] The author of "New England's Annoyances" obviously knew New England in the late 1630s and early 1640s; William Wood evidently did not. Besides, the William Wood who wrote spirits, good humor, and a touch of gay satire." He said that "The conclusion is characteristically Johnsonian with its abrupt change from satiric humor to utter seriousness. In any case, it was written by a man with much the same temperament and outlook as the author of the *Good News*. There are also striking verbal resemblances but whether Edward Johnson was the author or not, it is the earliest of our folk ballads and one of the very best." In his bibliography proper, Jantz was more cautious. He includes the poem not under Johnson's name but as the first of the anonymous poems, which are listed chronologically. Jantz says, "The internal evidence places the ballad in about the 1630s; in style, spirit and humor it bears some resemblance to Edward Johnson's Woburn verses and to the *Good News* of 1648."[15] Returning to the question in 1971, Jantz repeated the attribution:

> Variously in the *History*, especially in chapters xxiv and xxvii, there are what clearly seem to be allusions to or paraphrases of the first popular ballad of New England, one that was passed down by word of mouth and not transcribed and printed till the mid-eighteenth century. It was later called "Our Forefathers' Song" but is perhaps better called by its first three words, "New England's Annoyances." On grounds of style, content, and point of view it seems likely that Edward Johnson was the author. My first reconstruction and the first publication of the entire ballad appeared in Harrison T. Meserole's anthology, *Seventeenth-Century American Poetry* (1968). Since then further discovery and critical analysis of extant versions, and a crucial emendation, ventured by me, have carried the reconstruction farther toward completion, we hope.[16]

I follow Professor Jantz in believing that Johnson wrote "New England's Annoyances."

The general subject of New England's discommodities appears repeatedly in Johnson. The song's first specific complaint (stanza 1) concerns the scarcity of fruitful grass in New England's "wilderness wood." Johnson frequently characterizes New England as a "remote, rocky, barren, bushy, wild-woody wilderness" (210),[17] where it is necessary to cut "downe the woods" (84) to make way for farms. He characteristically refers to the colonization of New England as "Wilderness-work" (44, 51, 61, 70, 102, 114, 130, 145, 159, 165, 176, 189, 196, 231, 251, 253–54), and to Massachusetts as a "Wilderness" of "Wild and uncouth woods," although "Most men" have "an over-weaning desire . . . after Medow Land" (234). Like the song, Johnson's *History* associates the woods, the grass, and the cold: Johnson celebrates the Hartford area because it is "well stored with Meddow, which is greatly in esteeme with the people of New England, by reason the Winters are very long" (105–6; cf. 181, 190, 196–97, 234).

Stanzas 2 and 3 describe the bitter winters and the "violence" of the "north-wester" storms. Johnson too seems to take an almost perverse pleasure in New England's bitter winters. He recounts that in 1639–40, "the Lord *was pleased* [my italics] to send a very sharp winter, and more especially in strong storms of weekly snows, with very bitter blasts." Johnson seizes the opportunity to tell of a "servant maid" and a "Barber-Chiurgion" who froze to death, the latter being "more then ordinary laborious to draw men to . . . sinfull Errors" (191; cf. 45, 73, 84, 106). He disgustedly characterizes a group of malcontents who were dissatisfied with the winters: "They wanted a warmer country, and every Northwest wind that blew, they crept into some odd chimney-corner or other, to discourse of the diversity of Climates in the Southerne parts, but chiefly of a thing very sweet to the pallate of the flesh, called liberty" (207). Thus New England's winters function for Johnson as a metaphor for Calvinistic realities. New England winters are like the Puritan God—harsh but just; whereas Southern climates and pleasant summers symbolize a present worldly paradise—the snares of the devil. Johnson continues: the malcontents discourse of "liberty, which they suppose might be very easily attain'd, could they but once come into a place where all men were chosen to the office of a Magistrate, and all were preachers of the Word, and no hearers, then it would be all Summer and no Winter" (207–8; cf. 139).[18] Exactly the same mood underlies the wry humor of the song-writer's celebration of the cold: "if any's so hardy and will it withstand, / He forfeits a finger, a foot, or a hand." And Johnson, like the song-writer, refers to a "North-wester": "a cold North-west storme (which is the sharpest winde in this Country) freezing very vehemently" (92; cf. 73).

The transition in "New England's Annoyances" from the cold winters (stanzas 2 and 3) to the difficulties of raising corn (stanzas 4 and 5) focuses on the seasonal change ("When the ground opens we then take the hoe"). Johnson uses the same sequence. He describes the hard winter of 1632–33 ("a Terrible cold Winter, with weekly Snowes, and fierce Frosts betweene while congealing Charles River"), turns to the seasonal change ("The Winters Frost being extracted forth the Earth"), and describes the farmers' difficulties in planting the corn: "They fall to tearing up the Roots, and Bushes with their Howes. . . . Cutting down of the Woods, they inclose Corne fields. . . . The chiefest corne they planted before they had plowes was Indian Graine" (85). And when he thinks of those difficult days, Johnson, like the writer of "New England's Annoyances," turns to the celebration of pumpkins: "And let no man make a jest at Pumpkins, for with this fruit the Lord was pleased to feed his people to their good content, till Corne and Cattell were increased" (85).

Stanzas 6 (on currency), 7 and 8 (on clothing), and 9 and 10 (on food) constitute the major subjects of Johnson's Book 2, Chapter 21: "Of the suddain and unexpected fall of Cattel, and the great blessing of God in giving plenty of provision" (209). The key difference is that in the song, the scarcity of money seems to coexist with a scarcity of a variety of food, while in the *History*, Johnson focuses upon the abundance of food in contrast to its earlier scarcity.[19] Indeed, the very fact that the song is basically ahistorical, making it seem as if the starving time existed while currency and clothing were in short supply, points to Johnson's authorship, for historians have long complained about the factual inaccuracies of his *History*.[20] Johnson's Chapter 21 furnishes a good example of his inaccuracies. He dates the fall in the price of cattle as the spring of 1642, but it actually occurred in 1640. Johnson, the town recorder of Woburn, certainly knew *when* the bottom dropped out of the market in New England. He even began his poem on Woburn, which was founded in 1640, "In peniles age, I (Woburne Towne) began."[21] But the economic difficulties lasted for several years, and in his chronicle of the year 1640, Johnson was more interested in telling of "The great supply of godly Ministers for the good of his People in New England" (2, 16). So he put off the story of the collapse of the economy until he reached a more convenient time to discuss it. Further, in Book 2, Chapter 21, although he does tell of the scarcity of currency and clothing, he constantly shifts back to the 1630s, to mention the former scarcity of food, and turns forward to the late 1640s to tell of the colonists' present "plenty of cloathing." Johnson cares about the historical facts, but he wants to place them within a context that reveals (what he believes to be) their more important and more fundamental mythic truth.[22]

He opens the economic portrait of the early 1640s by describing the fall in the price of cattle, attributes it to the stop of immigration, and explains that the old hands had formerly purchased clothing, dainty foods, and a supply of money by selling their cattle to the new immigrants:

This Spring Cowes and Cattle of that kind (having continued at an excessive price so long as any came over with estates to purchase them) fell of a suddain in one week from 22 £ the Cow, to 6.7. or 8. £ the Cow at most, insomuch that it made all men admire how it came to pass, it being the common practice of those that had any store of Cattel, to sell every year a Cow or Two, which cloath'd their backs, fil'd their bellies with more varieties than the Country of it self afforded, and put gold and silver in their purses beside. (209)

Having briefly set forth the economic collapse, as well as its causes and consequences, Johnson goes on to emphasize New England's achievements—"a Nation to be born in a day, a Commonwealth orderly brought forth from a few Fugitives" (209). Johnson makes the economic depression the occasion for a celebration of New England's transformation:

> This remote, rocky, barren, bushy, wild-woody wilderness, a receptacle for Lions, Wolves, Bears, Foxes, Rockoones, Bags, Bevers, Otters, and all kind of wild creatures, a place that never afforded the Natives better then the flesh of a few wild creatures and parch't Indian corn incht out with Chesnuts and bitter Acorns, now through the mercy of Christ becom a second England for fertilness in so short a space, that it is indeed the wonder of the world; but being already forgotten of the very persons that tast of it at present, although some there be that keep in memory his mercies multitude, and declare it to their childrens children. (210)

And so the depression becomes an occasion not only for a celebration of the founders' achievement but also for a jeremiad, reminding later New Englanders of what the founders endured.

When Johnson brings up the scarcity of clothing (the subject of the song's stanzas 7 and 8), he emphasizes the present (c. 1650–51) supply: "For rayment, our cloth hath not been cut short, as but of late years the traders that way have encreased to such a number, that their shops have continued full all the year long" (211). He comments on the late extraordinary increase of sheep, and says that cloth is abundant "but the Farmers deem it better for their profit to put away their cattel and corn for clothing, then to set upon making of cloth." And, like the author of "New England's Annoyances" (stanzas 9 and 10), Johnson reminds his audience of the "want of food" in the early years. Johnson, however, emphasizes the abundance that accompanied the economic depression, and he dwells upon their present supply: "beside, flesh is now no rare food, beef, pork, and mutton being frequent in many houses, so that this poor Wilderness hath not only equalized England in food, but goes beyond it in some places for the great plenty of wine and sugar, which is ordinarily spent, apples, pears, and quince tarts instead of their former Pumpkin Pies" (210). Just as Johnson makes explicit the achievement of New Englanders to an English audience, so the author of "New England's Annoyances," in writing of "pumpkin at morning and pumpkin at noon" for a New England audience, is really recalling how New Englanders triumphed over their former "extream penury." New Englanders who first sang the song were currently (c. 1643) enjoying the "pottage and puddings and custards and pies" that they lacked in the early days. Johnson also contrasts English abundance with the colonists' deliberate choice of New England's scarcity. They left "Tables filled with great variety of Foode . . . Coffers filled with Coyne" and "Houses beautifully built and filled with all rech Furniture" in order to sail for "This yet untilled Wildernesse" (51). Johnson frequently recalls the scarcity experienced by the early settlers. "As for flesh they looked not for any in those times (although now they have plenty) unless they could barter with the Indians for Venison or Rockoons" (114; cf. 45, 91–92, 153–54, 182, and 256). In the same paragraph, he laments that "the want of English graine, Wheate, Barley and Rie proved a sore affliction to some stomacks, who could not live upon Indian Bread and water, yet were compelled to it till Cattell increased, and the Plowes could but goe: instead of Apples and Peares, they had Pomkins and Squashes of diverse kinds" (115). Compare "Instead of pottage and puddings and custards and pies, / Our pumpkins and parsnips are common supplies" (stanza 10). Johnson again seems to echo "New England's Annoyances" when he writes of the early settlers' dependence upon pumpkins; "let no man make a jest at Pumpkins [indirectly revealing that pumpkins *were* a common joke among the early New Englanders], for with this fruit the Lord was pleased to feed his people to their good content, till Corne and Cattell were increased" (85). Further, the passage in stanza 9 about clam banks' supplying "a delicate dish" has a counterpart where Johnson tells of the women going daily, "as the tide gave way . . . to the Mussells, and clambankes, which are a Fish as big as Horsemussells." Johnson records a supposed conversation between the women gathering food at the shore, one saying that her "Children are as cheerefull, fat, and lusty with feeding upon those Mussells, Clambanks and other Fish as they were in England, with their fill of Bread" (78).[23]

In that same chapter (2, 24) devoted to "the penuries of a Wilderness" (p. 75), Johnson celebrates the faithful who remained in

New England (contrasting them to the malcontents who supposed
"the present scarcity would never be turned into plenty" and who
therefore "removed themselves away, and so never beheld the great
good the Lord hath done for his people"). These faithful "in the
misse of beere supplied themselves with water." Later, describing
"the hard labours this people found in Planting this Wildernesse,"
Johnson comments on the settlers' "small pittance of Bread, if it
hold out," and ironically adds "but as for Drinke they have plenty,
the Countrey being well watered in all places that yet are found
out" (113). So, too, in stanzas 11 and 12 of the song, when barley is
"wanting to make into malt," the New Englanders make substitutes, and the author uses "spring water" as "my commonest
drink."

Stanza 13 of "New England's Annoyances" concerns the religious testimony necessary for admission into the church. Johnson's
entire history, which he evidently intended to entitle "The Wonder-Working Providences of Sion's Savior In New England,"[24] celebrates New England's theology. Johnson familiarly refers to the
literature of religious controversy (e.g., 91, 125, 136–39, 212, and
225). In his classic description of the formation of Woburn's
church, he states the necessity for the church applicant to give a
convincing spiritual relation:

> After the reverend Mr. Syms had continued in preaching and prayer
> about the space of four or five houres, the persons that were to joyn in
> Covenant, openly and professedly before the Congregation, and mes-
> sengers of divers Neighbour Churches . . . stood forth and first con-
> fessed what the Lord had done for their poor souls, by the work of his
> Spirit in the preaching of his Word, and Providences, one by one; and
> that all might know their faith in Christ was bottomed upon him, as he
> is revealed in his Word, and that from their own knowledg, they also
> declare the same, according to that measure of understanding the Lord
> had given them. (215–16)

He elsewhere justifies the testimony (29, 66, 213, 245) and here he
describes in detail how individuals become church members, while
putting the best possible interpretation ("all that is desired") upon
the necessity for a spiritual relation:

> the person desiours to joyn with the Church, cometh to the Pastor, and
> makes him acquainted therewith, declaring how the Lord hath been
> pleased to work his conversion, who discerning hopes of the persons
> faith in Christ, although weak, yet if any appear, he is propounded to

the Church in general for their approbation, touching his godly life and conversation, and then by the Pastor and some brethren heard again, who make report to the Church of their charitable approving of the person; but before they come to joyn with the Church, all persons within the Towne have publike notice of it, then publikely he declares the manner of his conversion, and how the Lord hath been pleased by the hearing of his Word preached, and the work of his Spirit in the inward parts of his soul, to bring him out of that natural darkness, which all men are by nature in and under, as also the measure of knowledg the Lord hath been pleased to indue him withal. And because some men cannot speak publikely to edification through bashfulness, the less is required of such, and women speak not publikely at all, for all that is desired, is to prevent the polluting the blessed Ordinances of Christ by such as walk scandalously, and that men and women to not eat and drink their own condemnation, in not discerning the Lords body. (217–18)

The final three stanzas of "New England's Annoyances" discuss malcontents and possible emigrants. Johnson does so repeatedly in *Good News From New England* and in his *History*. In *Good News*, he says "Yea male-contents none well content but discontentedly, / They breath out ill, being crost in will to all lamentingly" (6). In the *History*, he condemns the malcontents who in the first winter of 1630–31, fearing "poverty, and famishment, supposing the present scarcity would never be turned into plenty, removed themselves away" (77). Just as the author of the song censures the malcontents who "Find fault with our apples before they are mellow," Johnson uses fruit imagery to categorize those who object to New England's theology: "let me tell you friends you'l prove but trewants if you fall thus to Robbing of Orchards, and its an offence far beyond petty Larceny, to rob Christs Garden" (126; cf. the poem on p. 205). He recurs to the same pattern of thought and the same imagery when he compares the malcontents' early fears of starvation with the abundance of the 1640s: "and those who were formerly forced to fetch most of the bread they eat, and beer they drink, a hundred leagues by Sea, are through the blessing of the Lord so encreased, that they have not only fed their Elder Sisters, Virginia, Barbados, and many of the Summer Islands that were prefer'd before her for fruitfulness, but also the Grandmother of us all, even the fertile Isle of Great Britain" (247). Johnson also uses the lion-bear dichotomy of the fourteenth stanza's last line. Describing the preparations of the New Englanders for possible war against a foreign force, Johnson says: "Therefore let all people know that desire the downfal of New England, they are not to war against a people only exercised in feats of war, but men who are experienced in the deliverances of the Lord from the mouth of the Lion, and the paw of the Bear" (233).

The penultimate stanza makes the transition from the malcontents to the emigrants, "Now while some are going let others be coming." Johnson uses the "some . . . others" formula when describing the dismissal of some members from churches and the commendation of others (239; cf. 186). The metaphorical use of "while liquor is boiling it must have a scumming" seems not to occur in Johnson's writings—nor have I chanced to notice it elsewhere in New England's promotion literature.[25] But the concluding image in the stanza ("birds of a feather . . . are flocking together") has a counterpart in the *History* where Johnson condemns the rise of materialism and the "over-eager desire after the world" among New Englanders as an attempt by "every bird to feather his own nest" (260). Like Johnson's *Good News From New England*, the song concludes with an invitation to emigrate. The author of "New England's Annoyances" says that "you who the Lord intends hither to bring, / Forsake not the honey for fear of the sting," and Johnson, writing of the people who forsook Massachusetts during the economic depression of 1640–44, used the same imagery and association of ideas: "here grew a fulnesse in some, even to slight, if not loath the honey comb; many returned for England" (193). Just as the author of "New England's Annoyances" changes to the passive voice in the concluding quatrain in order to emphasize that God, not the emigrants, was really responsible for their coming to New England, so Johnson stresses that it is God who has brought the emigrant to New England. In 1628, Christ "raises an Army out of our English Nation" and "creates a New England to muster up the first of his Forces in" (23). And, of course, Johnson emphasized the bounty and blessings that the faithful found in New England throughout both his *Good News* and *History*.

Although the numerous individual thematic similarities (and a few verbal ones) make a good case for Johnson's authorship of "New England's Annoyances," I find the repeated association of the same ideas in both the song and Johnson's known writings especially significant. In the *History*, Book 1, Chapter 26, when Johnson tells "Of the gratious provisions the Lord made for his people," he concentrates on the hardships of the years 1632–33, mentioning most of the song's "annoyances." Johnson not only describes the difficulties in clearing the woods (82, 84, 85), the labor in planting crops (82, 84), the scarcity of English foods (82), and the winter's bitter cold (85), but also the abundance of fish (83), "Indian graine," and pumpkins (85). Again, in Book 1, Chapter 36, "Of the laborious worke Christ's people have in planting this wildernesse, set forth in the building the Towne of Concord, being the first in-land towne," Johnson tells how a trip through the wilderness wears out the settlers' "stockings to their bare skin in two or three houres" (112) and how the explorers had "small pittance of Bread" but plenty of "Drinke" because water was common (113). He describes the planters' tearing up "the Rootes and Bushes" with their hoes to make way for the first crops, tells of setting fish in with their corn, comments on the lack of "flesh" ("unless they could barter with the Indians for Venison or Rockoons"), and laments the scarcity of clothing, so that some "have been forced to go barefoot, and bareleg, till these latter dayes, and some in time of Frost and Snow" (114). Johnson explains that at the beginning of every new settlement the planters were reduced to poverty: they lacked flesh because the cattle died in the winter without good barns, the wolves killed the pigs, and "as for those who laid out their Estate upon Sheepe, they speed worst of any." At first there is no "English graine," only "Indian Bread and water," and instead of apples and pears, only "Pomkins and Squashes" (115). A third chapter in the *History* that gathers together many of song's motifs in Book 2, Chapter 21, "Of the suddain and unexpected fall of Cattel, and the great blessing of God in giving plenty of provision." The abundance of food during the economic depression causes Johnson to contrast that time (1640–44) both with the scarcity of the early years (1630–34) and with the present (1649–52) economic recovery. So he recalls that at the "first planting," the emigrants had no bread, no meat (although "flesh" is now "no rare food"), and no apples or pears (but only "their former Pumpkin Pies," 210). During the economic depression there was little clothing available and no "materials . . . to make it," but now the New Englanders have plenty of sheep, they are raising "hemp and flax," and the stores are "full all the year long" (211).

Johnson's *Good News From New England* also deals with the subjects of "New England's Annoyances." Like the song, *Good News* emphasizes the "rubs" (7, 15, 20), "hindrances" (23), and "grand complaint" (15) of New England. Johnson specifically dwells upon early hardships (6), scarcity of food (7), mosquitoes in summer (8), extreme cold in winter (9), failing economy (23), necessity to pay ministers in "*New Englands* pounds" (i.e., "currant pay") rather than in "old *England* Angells" (i.e., cash, 17), religious test for church membership (19, 20), and malcontents (6, 25). Despite dwelling on these "rubs," *Good News* primarily makes a sales pitch to those "who are like to reap benefite by transporting themselves" to New England (24), and closes with a memorable expression of the American Dream:

> Last, let all who desire to have themselves discovered to themselves, report to this place; where, if they seek not themselves they may find themselves, if not already lost in selfe-conceitednesse of some strong opinion, for which if they desire to be admired, let them leave this last long voyage, and keep at home. (25)

Johnson's invitation posits America as the opportunity for—and scene of—self-discovery and suggests that "this last long voyage" across the Atlantic to New England will bring the emigrant to paradise.

Besides the repetition of similar motifs and similar sequences, the same fundamental attitudes underlie the song and Johnson's known works. In the *History*, Johnson writes of the founding of Charlestown's church:

> This, as the other churches of Christ, began with a small number in a desolate and barren Wildernesse, which the Lord in his wonderful mercy hath turned to fruitfull Fields. Wherefore behold the present condition of these Churches compared with their beginnings; as they sowed in teares, so also have they Reaped in joy, and shall still so go on if plenty and liberty marre not their prosperity. (68)

If Plenty mar not their prosperity. This statement encapsulates the fundamental attitude of "New England's Annoyances." The celebration of winter's cold, the difficulties of growing corn, the scarcity of good food, the praise of water and poverty (clout upon clout)—all these details affirm a worldview that finds a true value in the hardships and poverty of New England's most difficult times. Johnson repeatedly expresses his absolute contempt for those who are more interested in material comfort than in spiritual light and who consequently "celebrate their Sabbaths in the chimney-corner" (253).[26] The "rubs," "hindrances," or "annoyances" of New England life are apt metaphors for Calvinistic theological realities. Johnson scorns the view of life as sensual lubberland and specifically condemns the *Book of Sports* by James I encouraging games after church. It urged "lewd and prophane persons to celebrate a Sabbath like the Heathen to Venus, Baccus and Ceres" (23). The "annoyances" affirm the basic realities of the spiritual world— which is the only New World, and which, in the imagination of the good New England Puritan, had its best worldly expression in their New World hardships. As Johnson said, "know this is the place where the Lord will create a new Heaven, and a new Earth in, new Churches, and a new Common-wealth together" (25).

It is a nineteenth- and twentieth-century commonplace that as the material wealth of colonial Americans increased, their religiousness decreased; spirituality is inversely proportional to materialism. What surprises us is that Johnson and the author of "New England's Annoyances" also thought so. The best statement of Johnson's attitude toward the founders' difficulties comes in the long first sentence of Book 2, Chapter 4, "Of the abundant mercies of Christ in providing liberall supply for his New England People, in regard of their outward man, Food, Rayment and all other necessaries and conveniences." Johnson paradoxically claims that great necessity makes men thankful for what they have:

> Now for the hardships on the left hand; they had as good an answer as in the former; their Christ had not saved their lives from the raging Seas to slay them in the Wildenesse with Famine; your life is much more pretious in the eyes of the Lord then food, and your bodies then rayment: yea, the Lord of Heaven, who hath honoured you so far as to imploy you in this glorious worke of his, knowes you must have these things, and it was not you, deare hearts, that chose this place, but the Lord, as seeing it most fit to doe his worke in, knowing that had you met with a Rich Land filled with all plenty, your heart would have been taken off this worke, which he must have done. (153–54)

I pointed out in chapter 2 that the author of "New England's Annoyances" evidently knew and echoed *New England's First Fruits.* Johnson did too. He echoes it and alludes to it several times in the *History* (202, 226, 264) and even discusses the Weld-Peters mission to England (262). Johnson displays the humor, literary ability, underlying philosophy, and characteristic habits of mind (e.g., the paradoxes and final serious turn) revealed in "New England's Annoyances." The *History* seemingly lacks one quality extremely important in the song, the presentation of both the speaker and the New Englanders as hicks. But the *History*, which was primarily intended for an English audience and which presented the achievements of New Englanders as heroic,[27] would not, of course, use the same strategies as a song aimed basically at a local audience. Conscious of the slur on New Englanders as Puritans who chose to flee rather than fight in England's Civil War, Johnson deliberately presents his New Englanders as "faithful Souldiers of Christ" (30).[28] But he also characterizes them as a "people wholly devoted to the Plow" (200), emphasizing that most New Englanders live by farming. In Wenham, Massachusetts, "the people live altogether upon husbandry, New England train'd up great store to this occupation" (226; cf. 237).[29]

Two other aspects of Johnson's view of Americans are more important, however, than the identification of New Englanders as farmers; and both are pertinent to the song's basic authorial attitudes. First, he repeatedly stresses the wilderness identification of America (88, 108, 111 [2], 113, 136, 145, and 211), colonization as "this Wilderness-work" (see my comment on the song's first complaint, above, p. 71), and New Englanders as "this Wilderness People" (87; cf. 100). He even metaphorically calls New Englanders "low Shrubs" in the American backwoods (60). Second, Johnson has a vision of New England and New Englanders as fulfilling a pattern of progress and accomplishment, rising from "low beginnings" (85) to a flourishing condition:

> But now behold the admirable Acts of Christ; at this his peoples landing, the hideous Thickets in this place were such, that Wolfes and Beares nurst up their young from the eyes of all beholders, in those very places where the streets are full of Girles and Boys sporting up and downe, with a continued concourse of people. Good store of Shipping is here yearly built, and some very faire ones: both Tar and Mastes the Countrey affords from its own soile; also store of Victuall both for their owne and Forreiners ships, who resort hither for that end: this town is the very Mart of the Land, French, Portugalls and Dutch come hither for Traffique. (71)

Johnson frequently emphasizes the progress of American civilization by portraying the original "low condition" of New Englanders who have since "been raised to much in a very little time" (198). He even writes the rags-to-riches version of the American Dream. Although some individuals have lost money in New England, "yet are there many hundreds of labouring men, who had not enough to bring them over [they came as servants], yet now worth scores, and some hundreds of pounds" (212). All three of these attitudes toward New Englanders and New England dominate "New England's Annoyances." The song explicitly presents New Englanders as

farmers and wilderness dwellers, and constantly implies the extraordinary achievement of New Englanders.[30]

Although Johnson frequently uses a Virgilian persona in the
History, he adopts a ritualistic abasement and refers to his poor
abilities and "rustic" situation whenever he calls attention to himself. He says that he cannot write the full history of all the theological errors because "besides the length of the discourse, there must
have been a more able Penman" (173). He apologizes for "medling
so meanly with such waighty matters, being blinded by eager affection, hee lost the sight of his great inability to the worke, when hee
first set Pen to Paper" (151). Johnson's very success in presenting
himself as an unworthy amateur has caused critics and historians to
scorn his literary ability. Johnson's superb control of tone—ranging
from the heroic and grandiose to the colloquial and familiar—is one
of the *History's* triumphs. Several recent critics have commented on
Johnson's success in creating a heroic myth of America, but his
success in creating colloquial dialogue such as that between the
"legal Pharises" (p. 126) is also remarkable.[31] The entire chapter
concerning theological errors (Chapter 40) attains a marvelous informal tone, partly because of the speaker's familiar address to the
reader and partly because the qualities he attributes to his reader
are identical with the narrator: e.g. "I'le tell you Friend, Neighbour, Brother, if you will" (125). The informal tone is also achieved
by the extreme familiarity of the comparisons, for the persons taking part in the dialogue are called presumptuous school boys robbing a farmer's orchards—and then Johnson extends this
identification of the "erronists" to his audience:

> By this discourse of theirs, you may see the manner how these Er-
> ronious, and Hereticall persons batter off the fruit from the goodly
> branches of Christs vines and make bare the flourishing trees planted in
> the house of the Lord, and yet professe themselves to be Schollars of
> the upper forme, that have learned as far as their Masters can teach
> them, but let me tell you friends you'l prove but trewants if you fall
> thus to Robbing of Orchards, and its an offence far beyond petty
> Larceny, to rob Christs Garden, let your pretences be what they will.
> (126)

Although Johnson repeatedly implies his (and the American)
identification with the backwoods, and although he describes his
own poetry as "a rustical rime" (205), the persona and the New
Englanders in the *History* are still not the hillbillies of "New En-

gland's Annoyances." But Johnson reveals both the ability and the tendency to create colloquial rustics. Indeed, two sensitive readers of Johnson who were not concerned with "New England's Annoyances" have remarked on just this aspect of Johnson's rhetorical strategy. William Frederick Poole commented in 1867 on Johnson's anticipation of James Russell Lowell's great rustic character of the midnineteenth century, Hosea Bigelow. And Cecilia Tichi notes that Johnson "implies a symbiotic relationship between Puritan minister and bushwacker," and that he "affirms a real and necessary relation between scriptural metaphor and New England hardscrabble."[32]

Johnson comes even closer to the rhetorical posture of "New England's Annoyances" in *Good News From New England*, where he pretends his audience is an Englishman named John and he, the speaker, an unlearned rustic. In the preface, he addresses "honest John," refers to his own "rustical harmony" that "rings but rudely," says he has borrowed "some Latine and Eloquent phrases . . . from others, as commonly clowns use to doe," and yet assures his reader that despite his humorous tone, "I am not in jest." He thrice calls his supposed reader "honest John" (ii, 6, 23), twice "my friend John" (14, 24), once "neighbour John" (22), and twice simply "John" (6 and 25). The effect is to portray the supposed audience as an honest man, a neighbor, and a friend—in short, the supposedly ordinary Englishman, a kind of local Everyman. Johnson further pretends that the speaker of *Good News* was formerly the same sort of person—but that he has become different by emigrating to America. The persona of *Good News* is out of touch and out of fashion. He was a rustic before, but he has become a backwoods hick during his American acculturation.[33] Therefore he requests that honest John "Favour my clown-ship if I prove too harsh" (ii). Although Johnson, in *Good News*, does not pretend that New Englanders are all yokels, he again demonstrates that he is capable of the manipulation of persona and audience displayed in "New England's Annoyances," and that he, like the author of the song, was aware of English condescension towards America and Americans.

Finally, I believe that the most puzzling single poem in Johnson's *History* suggests that he wrote "New England's Annoyances." The *History*'s penultimate poem is entitled "Of the wonder-working providences of Christ, wrought for his people among our English Nation, both in our Native country, and also in N. E. which should stir us up to mourn for all our miscarriages much the more" (257). The poem, in a traditional religious genre, penitential verse, consists of twenty-two stanzas, each having six lines of iambic pentameter, rhyming *ababcc*. Prose commentaries after stanzas 4, 7, 13, 15, and 22 apply the poem to events in New England. Suitably, the poem's title paraphrases Johnson's intended title for his book, for the poem serves as the book's coda, repeating in microcosm much of the *History*.[34] But surprisingly, Johnson borrows the first four stanzas from a popular English poem entitled *The Passion of a Discontented Mind* (1601). Although usually attributed to Nicholas Breton, the poem has recently been ascribed to Robert Devereux, second earl of Essex (1566–1601). It had three separate editions (1601, 1602, and 1621) and was also adapted by G. Ellis in *The Lamentation of the Lost Sheep* (London: Jaggard, 1605). Most important, John Dowland used it as song number ten in his great song collection, *A Pilgrimes Solice* (London, 1612).[35] Since Johnson prints the first four stanzas (making seventeen substantive changes)[36] of *The Passion of a Discontented Mind*, his source cannot have been Ellis, who drastically changed the poem, or Dowland, who copies only stanzas 1, 2, and 11.

But why did Johnson borrow any stanzas? He applies—or attempts to apply—them to New England and to his own purposes with the last part of his title ("which should stir us up to mourn for all our miscarriages much the more") and with the following note: "The consideration of the wonderful providence of Christ in planting his N.E. Churches, and with the right hand of his power preserving, protecting, favouring, and feeding them upon his tender knees: Together with the ill requital of his all-infinite and undeserved mercies bestowed upon us hath caused many a soul to lament for the dishonor done to his Name, and fear of his casting of[f] this little handful of his, and the insulting of the enemy, whose sorrow is set forth in these four first staffs of verses" (257–58). Despite Johnson's attempted application, these opening stanzas of "Wonder-Working Providences" do not seem to belong in Johnson's *History*. They have a self-pitying note (e.g.: "The wound fresh bleeding must be stanch'd with tears, / Tears cannot come unless some grief proceed") and are—to a sensitive critic such as Harold Jantz—obviously not by Johnson.[37] The stanzas borrowed from *The Passion of a Discontented Mind* simply do not match the style, tone, and themes of the rest of the poem. In the structure of the whole book, Johnson's penultimate poem, "Of the wonder-working providences," serves the purpose of a humble, penitential appeal to God, for the *History* concludes with a triumphant poem ("Oh King of Saints") announcing that God had come to call forth the Puritans to

battle for the millenium (272–75). The sorrowfulness and repent-
ance of the penultimate poem is both rhetorically and religiously
sound, but, Johnson could easily achieve this tone without borrow-
ing, as the penultimate stanza "Of the wonder-working providences
of Christ" makes clear:

> Lord, stay thy hand, thy Jacobs number's small,
>   Powre out thy wrath on Antichrists proud Thrones;
> Here [hear] thy poor flocks that on thee daily call,
>   Bottle their tears, and pity their said groans.
> Where shall we go, Lord Christ? we turn to thee,
> Heal our back-slidings, forward press shall we.

(261)

Why borrow those stanzas? I believe the reason is that Johnson
wanted his readers to recognize the poem as a song. Dowland was,
after all, the most popular songwriter of his day. His songs, according to William Barclay Squire, writing at the end of the nineteenth
century, were "still sung more than the compositions of any other
Elizabethan composer."[38] And song no. ten, from the collection *A
Pilgrimes Solace* (a title certain to appeal to the Puritans)[39] was (according to the standard authority on Dowland) among his very best
tunes.[40] Thus, Johnson probably knew the song and expected his
audience to know it.[41] The poem summarizes the contents and
presents the theme of the *History*. Johnson evidently hoped that his
poem "Of the wonder-working providences of Christ" would become a popular New England song. . . . Who knows? Perhaps it
did.

Although good records exist for seventeenth-century New England literature, precious few songs survive from the early days.
The psalms, of course, are the great exception, but where are the
secular songs? Thomas Morton's Maypole song[42] and "New England's Annoyances" are the only ones that come to mind. From a
few seventeenth-century commonplace books and researches of the
folklorists, we know that New Englanders sang the old ballads.[43]
With the probable exception of Johnson, and with the certain exception of the author of "New England's Annoyances," no first-
generation New England Puritan wrote secular songs that survive.
In the next generation, Michael Wigglesworth used the ballad
stanza for his popularization of New England theology, *The Day of
Doom* (1662)—a best-seller in England and New England. As I
suggested elsewhere, this fine poem passed into the oral tradition

and probably was transformed during the nineteenth century into the spiritual "Sinner Man."[44] If I am correct that Johnson incorporated the popular song "From silent night, true register of moans" into his poem "Of the wonder-working providences of Christ" in order to indicate that his summary poem was a song, then, I think, one more bit of evidence exists for believing that Johnson wrote "New England's Annoyances."

Lacking external evidence, I cannot conclude that Johnson wrote America's earliest extant folk song. But if Johnson did not write it, there must have existed another first-generation New England Puritan who wrote good poetry and who had exactly Johnson's literary ability, habits of mind, playfulness, ultimate fundamental seriousness, and ideological characteristics. Perhaps another such Puritan flourished in New England in the 1630s and 1640s; but I believe that there was only one and that Edward Johnson wrote "New England's Annoyances."

Appendixes
Textual Considerations

1. The 1758 Version

The earliest extant text of "New England Annoyances"[1] appears in Benjamin Mecom's chapbook, *Father Abraham's Speech* (Boston: B. Mecom, 1758). *Father Abraham's Speech* is the early title for *The Way to Wealth*. Benjamin Franklin composed *The Way to Wealth* during the summer of 1757 as a preface to *Poor Richard Improved: Being an Almanac . . . for . . . 1758* (Philadelphia: Franklin and Hall, [1757]).[2] Evidently Mecom, Franklin's nephew, judged the preface a good possibility for separate publication, so he featured it in the early spring of 1758, appending to it "seven curious Pieces of Writing."[3] The table of contents thus identified the chapbook's penultimate piece: "An Old Song, wrote *by one of our first* New England *Planters, on their Management in those* good *Old* Times. *To the Tune of* a Cobler there was, etc." In this text (hereafter called *A* text), the song consists of eleven numbered quatrains. Eighteen of the forty-four lines in *A* text are unique: they have no counterpart in the song as printed in such standard nineteenth-century anthologies as Rufus Wilmot Griswold's *The Poets and Poetry of America* (1842) or Evert A. and George L. Duyckinck's *Cyclopaedia of American Literature* (1855).[4] And the remaining twenty-six lines, although similar to those in the nineteenth-century texts, differ in numerous substantive details. Moreover, the previously known texts all contain some lines not in *A* text. The text itself, therefore, confirms what the title reveals: this is a folk song, recorded from oral tradition rather than from printed copies of the original.[5] Here is Mecom's text:

An old Song. —Tune, *A Cobler there was.*

1. FROM the End of *November* till three Months are gone,
The Ground is all frozen as hard as a Stone,

And our great Mountains, above and below,
Are often-times cover'd with Ice and with Snow.

   2. And when the Ground opens we then take a Hoe,   5
And make the Ground ready to plant and to sow;
But Corn being planted, and Seed being sown,
The Worms eat much of it before it is grown.

   3. While it is a growing much Spoil there is made
By Birds and by Squirrels that pluck up the Blade;   10
And when it is grown to full Corn in the Ear,
It's apt to be spoil'd by Hog, Racoon, and Deer.

   4. Our Money's soon counted, for we have just none,
All that we brought with us is wasted and gone.
We buy and sell Nothing but upon Exchange,   15
Which makes all our Dealings uncertain and strange.

   5. And now our Apparel begins to grow thin,
And Wool is much wanted to card and to spin.
If we get a Garment to cover without,
Our innermost Garment is Clout upon Clout.   20

   6. Our Cloth it is *boughten*, it's apt to be torn,
It need to be clouted before it is worn.
For clouting our Garments does injure us Nothing:
Clouts double are warmer than single whole Cloathing.

   7. And of our green Corn-Stalks we make our *best* Beer,   25
We put it in Barrels to drink all the Year:
Yet I am as healthy, I verily think,
Who make the Spring-Water my commonest Drink.

   8. And we have a Cov'nant one with another,
Which makes a Division 'twixt Brother and Brother: 30
For some are rejected, and others *made* SAINTS,
Of those that are *equal* in Virtues and Wants.

   9. For such like Annoyance we've many mad Fellows,
Find Fault with our Apples before they are mellow;
And they are for ENGLAND, they will not stay here,   35
But *Meet with a Lion in shunning a Bear.*

   10. But while such are going, let others be coming.
Whilst Liquors are boiling, they should have a Scumming:
And I cannot blame 'em, since *Birds of a Feather*
Are chusing their Fellows by flocking together.   40

   11. But you that THE LORD intends hither to bring,
Forsake not your Honey *for Fear of a* Sting:
But bring both a quiet and contented Mind,
And all *needful* Blessings you surely shall find.

The eighteen lines without counterpart in the previously known texts are: 1–2 (on weather), 13–16 (on currency), 25–28 (on drink), 29–32 (on religion), and 33–36 (on emigration). Ten of these unique lines are on topics (weather, drink, and emigration) found in the standard versions and complement those texts. Indeed, these lines not only complement but also complete the other texts. As I will show below, the progress of thought is more logical when *A* text is added to the traditional texts. And even the structure of the song calls for these ten lines to be added to the usual texts, since two quatrains are typically devoted to each "annoyance." On the other hand, the quatrains on currency and religion (13–16 and 29–32, respectively) concern subjects different from those in the standard texts. The question naturally arises whether these stanzas belong with the original poem. I believe they do, for they are indubitably examples of "New England's Annoyances," common subjects of complaint in the 1640s. Although currency and religion remained problems in New England throughout the colonial period, they were especially troublesome in the early period. After Massachusetts issued its own currency in the late seventeenth century, bartering was no longer quite so necessary or so common.[6] And, although revisionist historians have sometimes denied the obvious, religious differences generally became less crucial by the eighteenth century.[7] These two topics, however, were major issues in the 1640s, often reflected in New England promotion and antipromotion literature. Therefore, I believe that these two subjects were part of the original song and that, in the process of oral transmission, they were dropped from one version.

As I will show below, all but one of the nineteenth-century versions of "New England's Annoyances" descend directly or indirectly from the text entitled "Our Forefather's Song," printed in the *Massachusetts Magazine* 3 (January 1791): 52–53. This text (hereafter called *C* text) consists of forty-six lines, including a prefatory couplet. *A* text is not the source of *C* text, for *C* text contains twenty unique lines: 1–4 (introduction), 7–10 (weather), 27–34 (food), and 35–38 (drink). All these subjects complement those in *A* text. The inescapable conclusion is that both *A* and *C* texts descend from the original song and that these two texts represent different lines of oral transmission.

In addition to the actual contents of the lines, *A* text yields two exciting new bits of information: the quatrain arrangement and the tune. The other three earliest texts all attempted to print the poem in octaves, probably because eight lines each were devoted to three major subjects in those texts. Although two nineteenth-century scholars (Alonzo Lewis in 1829 and William Shaw Russell in 1846) arranged the poem in quatrains, they did so either by omitting the first couplet (Lewis) or by printing it as introductory (Russell). Not only are all the lines in *A* text arranged in logical quatrain form, but, when the unique lines in *A* text are added to the other texts, they allow the resulting reconstructed version to be composed entirely of well-wrought quatrains. The information that the song was sung *"To the Tune of* A Cobler there was, etc." identifies the tune as an old English folk tune, best known as the "Derry down" melody. Richard Leveridge's version, arranged for John Gay's song "A Cobler There Was" in *The Beggar's Opera*, became the best-known eighteenth-century version of the "Derry down" folk song in England and America.[8] Although eighteenth-century New Englanders evidently sang "New England's Annoyances" to Leveridge's arrangement, it is anachronistic to use that name and arrangement rather than "Derry down."[9] One perceptive nineteenth-century authority realized that the common folk tune "Derry down" suited the anapestic tetrameter line and quatrain arrangement of "New England's Annoyances." In 1846, William Shaw Russell noted that "a musical friend informs us that these popular lines would find appropriate music in the old tune of *Derry Down*."[10] The evidence of *A* text conclusively proves that the poem was originally written in quatrains and originally sung to "Derry down."

2. The 1774, 1791, and 1822 Versions

In 1970, while compiling a bibliography of the periodical verse of the American Revolution, I came across another text of "New England's Annoyances" in the "Poets Corner" (p. 4, col. 1) of Isaiah Thomas's (Boston) *Massachusetts Spy*, for 3 February 1774 (hereafter cited as *B* text). It is extremely similar to *C* text and to the nineteenth-century printings of the folk song. Since, as I will argue below, *B* text is as authentic as the better-known *C* text, I will print it here:

For the MASSACHUSETTS SPY.

Mr. THOMAS,
  Please to give the following lines a place in Poets Corner, *and you will oblige one who wishes we had no greater* annoyances *at this day. It is an old ballad composed and sung by some of the first settlers of New-England, called* New-England's annoyances, *recollected and repeated lately, by an old*

lady of 92 years of age; it may serve to show, not the elegance of the Poet, but some of the hardships, fare *and* patience *of the first settlers of this country.*

NEW-England's annoyances you that would know them
Pray ponder these verses which briefly do show them;
The place where we live is a wilderness wood,
Where grass is much wanting that's fruitful and good:
Our mountains and hills and valleys below   5
Being commonly cover'd with ice and with snow,
And when the north-wester with violence blows
Then every man pulls his cap over his nose;
But if any are so hardy and will it withstand,
He forfeits a finger, a foot or a hand.   10

When the spring opens we then take the hoe
And make the ground ready to plant and to sow;
Our corn being planted and seed being sown,
The worms destroy much before it is grown;
And when it is growing, some spoil there is made,   15
By birds and by squirrels that pluck up the blade,
Even when it is grown to full corn in the ear,
It is often destroyed by racoons and deer.

And now our garments begin to grow thin,
And wool is much wanted to card and to spin;   20
If we can get a garment to cover without,
Our other in-garments are clout upon clout;
Our clothes we brought with us are often much torn,
They need to be clouted before they are worn;
But clouting our garments they hinder us nothing,   25
Clouts double are warmer than single whole cloathing.

If flesh meat be wanting to fill up our dish,
We have carrets and pumkins and turnips and fish;
And when we have a mind for a delicate dish,
We repair to the *clam-bank* and there we catch fish.   30
Instead of pottage and puddings and custards and pies,
Our pumkins and parsnips are common supplies;
We have pumkin at morning, and pumkin at noon,
If it was not for pumkins we should be *undoon.*

If barley be wanting to make into malt,   35
We must be contented, and think it no fault,
For *we* can make liquor to sweeten our lips,
Of pumkins and parsnips and walnut-tree chips.

Now while some are going let others be coming,
For while liquor is boiling it must have a scumming,   40
But we will not blame them, for birds of a feather,
By seeking their fellows are flocking together.
But you who the LORD intends hither to bring,

Forsake not the honey for fear of the sting,
But bring both a quiet and contented mind   45
And all needful blessings you surely will find.

In addition to the text itself, the most valuable detail furnished by the 1774 printing is that the poem's title is "New England's Annoyances." No title was given in *A* text or in any later authoritative text. The usual nineteenth-century title, "Our Forefather's Song" (first used as the title in *C* text, 1791) is obviously anachronistic. The title "New England's Annoyances" is perfect. It is justified not only by the song's opening line and by the echo of the opening of the fourteenth stanza (I refer here to the reconstructed version), but also by its apt characterization of the poem's subject. Later critics appreciated its suitability as a title even without the authority of *B* text. William C. Burton (who evidently used Griswold's version of *C* text) called it "New England's Annoyances" in 1858 (as did John W. S. Hows in 1865, W. J. Linton in 1878, and James Barr in 1891—all following Burton). And Albert Matthews in 1916, after discovering *B* text, adopted the title "New England's Annoyances." I believe it was originally the song's title. I might also point out that the source for the poem in 1774 was "an old lady of 92 years of age," who seems to grow younger as years pass.

The *Massachusetts Magazine* text (*C* text) is listed as the earliest known text by the standard authorities.[11] It was the source (direct or indirect) of nearly all other published versions of "New England's Annoyances." Here follows the text from the *Massachusetts Magazine* 3 (January 1791): 52–53:

To the EDITORS *of the* MASSACHUSETTS MAGAZINE.
   GENTLEMEN,
The following song is upwards of one hundred and sixty years old. The British are passionately attached to the remains of their ancient poetry. I wish to encourage a similar spirit in America.   Yours, J. F.

New England's annoyances you that would know them,
Pray ponder these verses which briefly doth shew them.

Our Forefather's SONG
Composed about the year 1630.

I.

The place where we live is a wilderness wood,
Where grass is much wanting that's fruitful and good:
Our mountains and hills and our vallies below,   5
Being commonly covered with ice and with snow:
And when the northwest wind with violence blows,

Then every man pulls his cap over his nose:
But if any's so hardy and will it withstand,
He forfeits a finger, a foot, or a hand.   10

II.

But when the spring opens we then take the hoe,
And make the ground ready to plant and to sow;
Our corn being planted and seed being sown,
The worms destroy much before it is grown;
And when it is growing some spoil there is made,   15
By birds and by squirrels that pluck up the blade;
And when it is come to full corn in the ear,
It is often destroyed by racoon and by deer.

III.

And now our garments begin to grow thin,
And wool is much wanted to card and to spin;   20
If we can get a garment to cover without,
Our other in garments are *clout upon clout;
Our clothes we brought with us are apt to be torn,
They need to be clouted soon after they're worn,
But clouting our garments they hinder us nothing,   25
Clouts double, are warmer than single whole clothing.

IV.

If fresh meat be wanting, to fill up our dish,
We have carrots and pumpkins and turnips and fish;
And is there a mind for a delicate dish
We repair to the clam banks, and *there* we catch fish.   30
Instead of pottage and puddings and custards and pies,
Our pumpkins and parsnips are common supplies;
We have pumpkins at morning and pumpkins at noon;
If it was not for pumpkins we should be undone.

V

If barley be wanting to make into malt,   35
We must be contented and think it no fault;
For we can make liquor to sweeten our lips,
Of pumpkins and parsnips and walnut tree chips.
†Now while some are going let others be coming,
For while liquor's boiling it must have a scumming;   40
But I will not blame them, for birds of a feather,
By seeking their fellows are flocking together.

---

*Clout signifies patching

†*The above, was taken memoriter, from the lips of an old Lady, at the advanced period of 92. There is visibly a break in the sense, commencing at the 5th line of the 5th verse:* We conceive that four lines have been lost; and are also of opinion that the four last lines of the 5th verse, and all of the 6th belong together. Perhaps some *poetical antiquarian* may favour us with a correcter edition.

VI

But you whom the lord intends hither to bring,
Forsake not the honey for fear of the sting;
But bring both a quiet and contented mind,   45
And all needful blessings you surely will find.

In his prefatory note, the contributor ("J. F.")[12] who sent in the poem stresses his patriotic motivation. Since the English collect their old ballads ("J. F." no doubt had in mind Bishop Percy's *Reliques of Ancient English Poetry* and James MacPherson's Ossianic poems), he wants the Americans to do likewise. He therefore emphasizes the song's antiquity ("upwards of one hundred and sixty years old"), gives it the anachronistic title "Our FOREFATHER'S SONG," and adds the oft-repeated statement "Composed about the year 1630." He also tries to make sense of the song's stanzaic structure, but he forces it into octaves by printing the first couplet as an epigraph, thus leading several nineteenth-century editors into the mistake of omitting that couplet. It may be, however, that "J. F." carefully follows the text given him. He faithfully prints the fifth octave of the poem as an octave and the final stanza as a quatrain, despite his own acute critical observation: "*There is visibly a break in the sense, commencing at the 5th line of the 5th verse:* We conceive that four lines have been lost; and are also of opinion that the four last lines of the 5th verse, and all of the 6th belong together." Or it may be that the magazine's editor added this observation, since the last sentence, requesting "a correcter edition," is clearly editorial.

The source for *C* text is evidently the same as for *B* text. In 1774, the song had been "*recollected and repeated lately, by an old lady of* 92 *years of age.*" Here in 1791, we learn that the song "*was taken memoriter, from the lips of an old Lady, at the advanced period of* 92." Even without these details concerning the informant, I would suspect that *B* and *C* texts have the same source because they are nearly identical. What, then, is their relationship? Is *C* text merely a copy of *B* text? Can their differences be accounted for by speculating that some "improving" editor has produced *C* text from *B*? Two substantive variants between *B* and *C* texts support this hypothesis. The most obvious attempt to correct *C* text occurs in line 27. The couplet in *B* text reads:

If flesh meat be wanting to fill up our dish,
We have carrets and pumkins and turnips and fish;

                                        (27–28)

C text substitutes "fresh" for "flesh." The change might seem to a modern reader to make better sense of the line—but it weakens the couplet's meaning. More significant, it is the kind of change someone would make who was trying to improve the text but did not know that the primary meaning of *meat* through the midseventeenth century was "food." The person who tampered with *C* text probably thought "flesh meat" was redundant, and so made his anachronistic "improvement."

Until I wrote the authorship chapter in 1981, I believed that an improving editor had attempted to make *C* text seem quaint and *oulde.* The first couplet in *B* text reads:

> NEW-England's annoyances you that would know them
> Pray ponder these verses which briefly do show them;
>
> (1–2)

In line 2, *C* text has "doth" instead of "do." Since most early-seventeenth-century writers use "do" rather than an antique "doth," I thought the original probably read "do." But Edward Johnson characteristically prefered "doth" in his writings.[13] So I have reconsidered this supposed bit of evidence. However, a second anachronistic detail is found in line 43, where some fussy grammarian has imposed late-eighteenth-century standards on the song. The couplet in *B* text reads:

> But you who the LORD intends hither to bring,
> Forsake not the honey for fear of the sting,
>
> (43–44)

For *B* text's "who," *C* text has "whom." Based upon these two substantive variants (flesh/fresh and who/whom) between *B* and *C* texts, upon the prefatory material, and upon the octave arrangement of the stanzas, I conclude that some would-be "improver" has tampered with *C* text.

Despite the evidence of editorial "improvements" in *C* text, I must reject the hypothesis that *C* text is merely an "improved" copy of *B*. I reason that *A* text, with its entirely different line of descent from the original song, can serve as a guide to the possible authenticity of texts *B* and *C*. Here follows a table (keyed to the line numbers of texts *B-C*) of the substantive differences between *B* and *C* texts when the comparable line exists in *A* text:

A—*Father Abraham's Speech* (Boston 1758)
B—*Mass. Spy* 3 February 1774, 4/1
C—*Mass. Magazine* 3 (January 1791): 52–53

B–C Variants, Compared with A

11 And when *A*	When *B*; But when *C*
17 (1) And when *A, C*	Even when *B*
17 (2) grown *A, B*	come *C*
18 (1) racoon *A, C*	racoons *B*
18 (2) and deer *A, B*	and by deer *C*
23 apt to be *A, C*	often much *B*
24 before A, B	soon after *C*
41 I *A, C*	we *B*
43 that *A,*	who *B*; whom *C*

Examining the table, we see that in three instances (17 [2], 18 [2], and 24), *B* text agrees with *A*. In four instances (17 [1], 18 [1], 23, and 41), *C* text agrees with *A*. And in two instances (11 and 43), all three texts differ. The substantive differences strongly suggest that *B* and *C* texts have equal claim to authority. Moreover, the nature of one variant (23 "often much" [*B*] or "apt to be" [*C*]) proves in itself that *C* text has a different claim to authority than *B* text. For "apt to be" seems to me clearly superior to "often much," which, I think, has been corrupted while in the oral tradition by the memorial influence of "much" (14 and 20) and "often" (18). The alternative "apt to be" (confirmed by *A* text) avoids the deadening repetition and is therefore superior. Further, I judge it unlikely that an "improver" of *B* text would have thought it desirable to change "often much"—and, if he had I think it again extraordinarily unlikely that he would have come up with "apt to be." (In my opinion, "commonly" would be the more likely choice.)

I conclude that texts *B-C* were taken down at different times from the same informant, that she evidently sang the song (or simply repeated it) slightly differently on the two occasions, and that both texts therefore have nearly identical claims to authority, although *C* text has probably been tampered with by some editor.

One final text has similar claims to authority and must be derived from the same informant. This hitherto-unknown version appeared in the Plymouth, Massachusetts, newspaper, *The Old Colony Memorial*, 18 May 1822, pp. 1–2 (*D* text). Allen Danforth, the printer (and also, I presume, the editor) of the newspaper had the instincts of a scholar and presented, evidently, all the information he possessed concerning the song:

[We have no other tradition, respecting the following lines, than is derived from the letter, published beneath from Dr. Waterhouse to the late Deacon Spooner,[14] dated in 1817. They are venerable for antiquity and truth, tho' not distinguished for refinement and invention.]

The hardships and fare of the first planters of New-England.

An old song One Hundred and fifty years ago.

New-England's annoyances you that would know them,
Pray ponder these verses, which briefly does show them,
The place where we live, is a wilderness wood,
Where grass is much wanted, that's fruitful and good.
Our mountains and Hills and Valleys below   5
Being commonly covered with frost and with snow.
And when the North-West wind with violence blows,
Then every man pulls his cap over his nose.
But if any are so hardy, and will it withstand,
He forfeits a finger, a foot, or a hand.   10

2. When the spring opens, we then take the hoe,
And make the ground ready to plant and to sow,
Our corn being planted, and seed being sown,
The worms destroy much before it is grown,
And when it is growing, some spoil there is made,   15
By birds and by squirels, who pluck up the blade,
Even when it is grown to full corn in the ear,
It is often destroyed by Racoon and Deer.

3. And now our garments, begin to grow thin
And wool is much wanted to card and to spin,   20
If we *can* get a garment to cover *without*,
Our other *in*-garments, are clout upon clout,
Our cloaths we brought with us, are apt to be torn
They need to be clouted soon after they are worn,
But clouting our garments, they hinder us nothing,   25
Clouts double, are warmer, than single whole clothing.

4. If flesh meat be wanting to fill up our dish,
We have Carrots and Pumpkins, & Turnips, & Fish,
And if we have a mind for a delicate dish,
We repair to the clam-bank, and *there* we catch Fish.   30

Instead of pottage and puddings and custards and pyes,
Our pumpkins and parsnips are common supplies,
We have pumpkin at morning, and pumkin at noon,
If it was not for pumpkin we should be undoon*.

---

*As they then pronounced *undone*.
Repeated by an old lady 94 years old in 1767.

If Barley be wanting to make into malt 35
We must be contented, and think it no fault;
For we can make liquor to sweeten our lips
Of pumpkin and parsnips and walnut tree chips.

6. Now while some are going let others be coming,
For while liquor is boiling, it must have a scumming. 40
But I will not blame them, for Birds of a feather,
By seeking their fellows are flocking together.

But you, who the Lord intends hither to bring
Forsake not the honey for fear of the sting
But bring both a quiet and contented mind 45
And all needful blessings you surely shall find.

Cambridge, 15 December, 1817

Dear & very respected Sir,
I here send you a curiosity; which I hope, and believe, will gratify your friends and townsmen at their approaching anniversary of the landing of our Forefathers. It is a poetical description of the *hard fare* of our Progenitors soon after they landed on your renowned shore.

Who the author was I know not; nor do I *when* it was written; neither have I been informed who the old lady was who repeated these verses in 1767, when 94 years of age. To me it is probable that they were taken down from her mouth, like the ancient poems of Ossian, in Scotland.

This paper was given to me by the late Madam Bowdoin, the worthy wife of my excellent and intimate friend GOVERNOR BOWDOIN. I send them to *you* as a pleasant relic; not merely because I regard you the Father of the Town where you reside, but as a mark of that respectful and steady friendship so long subsisting between you and your kinsman,

BENJAMIN WATERHOUSE.

The numbering of the stanzas, the attempt to print them as octaves, and the uncertainty about where the fourth stanza ends and the fifth begins—all suggest that whoever wrote down this poem was influenced by *C* text's octave arrangement and its editorial note on the relationship between the final two stanzas. However, except for the three quatrain divisions (following the octave numbered "4") and the numbering of the stanzas (which omits the number 5), the arrangement is exactly the same as that of *B* text. Further, the title *"The hardships and fare of the first planters of New-England"* paraphrases the last part of *B* text's introduction *("the hardships, fare and patience of the first settlers of this country")*. To judge by the prefatory material, one would think that *D* text must be based upon *B* text. But Madame Elizabeth (Erving) Bowdoin,

who gave Dr. Waterhouse the poem, must have been familiar with
C text since an extended obituary of her husband, Governor James
Bowdoin, appeared in the same issue of the *Massachusetts Magazine*
that contained *C* text.[15] Nevertheless, the text itself differs from
both *B* and *C* texts, and the specific information that the source was
an "old lady 94 years old in 1767" (no year was given for her age of
92 in either *B* or *C* texts) has an authentic ring. The following table
of substantive variants among texts *B-D* demonstrates their close
relationship.

Substantive Variants, B-D

2	do *B*	doth *C;* does *D*	
4	wanting *B, C*	wanted *D*	
5	valleys *B, D*	our vallies *C*	
6	ice *B, C*	frost *D*	
7	north-wester *B*	northwest wind *C, D*	
9	any are *B, D*	any's *C*	
11	When *B, D*	But when *C*	
16	that *B, C*	who *D*	
17(1)	Even when *B, D*	And when *C*	
17(2)	grown *B, D*	come *C*	
18(1)	racoons *B*	racoon *C, D*	
18(2)	deer *B, D*	by deer *C*	
23	often much *B*	apt to be *C, D*	
24(1)	before *B*	soon after *C, D*	
24(2)	they are *B, D*	they're *C*	
27	flesh *B, D*	fresh *C*	
29	when we have *B*	is there a *C;* if we have *D*	
30	clam-bank *B, D*	clam banks *C*	
33	pumkin . . . pumkin *B, D*	pumkins . . . pumkins *C*	
34(1)	pumkins *B, C*	pumkin *D*	
34(2)	*undoon B, D*	undone *C*	
38	pumpkins *B, C*	pumpkin *D*	
40	liquor is *B, D*	liquor's *C*	
41	we *B*	I *C, D*	
43	who *B, D*	whom *C*	
46	will *B, C*	shall *D*	

    The above table shows that *D* text agrees with *B* but differs from
C in thirteen instances (5, 9, 11, 17[1], 17[2], 18[2], 24[2], 27, 30,
33, 34[2], 40, and 43). Second, *D* agrees with *C* but differs from *B*
in five instances (7, 18[1], 23, 24[1], and 41). Third, *D* does not
agree with either *B* or *C* in eight instances: in six *B* and *C* agree (4,
6, 16, 34[1], 38, and 46); and in two, all three texts differ (2, 29).

    One other table may shed some light on *D* text's relationship to
B-C. How do the substantive variants among all the *B-D* texts
compare with *A?*

B-D Variants, Compared with A

6	ice	A, B, C	frost	D
11	When	B, D	And when	A; But when C
16	that	A, B, C	who	D
17(1)	Even when	B, D	And when	A, C
17(2)	grown	A, B, D	come	C
18(1)	racoons	B	racoon	A, C, D
18(2)	deer	A, B, D	by deer	C
23	often much	B	apt to be	A, C, D
24	before	A, B	soon after	C, D
41	we	B	I	A, C, D
43	who	B, D	that	A; whom C
46	shall	A, D	will	B, C

In only one instance (46) does *D* text disagree with both *B* and *C* and agree with *A*. The relevant couplet in *A* reads:

> But bring both a quiet and contented Mind,
> And all *needful* Blessings you surely shall find.

Both *B* and *C* texts conclude "will find" instead of "shall find." The difference between "shall" *(A* and *D)* and "will" *(B* and *C)* is not forceful enough to make me believe either first, that "shall" must have been in the original and that therefore *D* text must be authentic (even though I do slightly prefer "shall" to "will" and suspect that it was in the original), or second, that "shall" is so different from "will" that a singer/reciter of the poem might not have accidentally, in the process of oral transmission, substituted by chance the original for the alternative word.

Another way of verifying *D* text's possible authenticity is to examine its unique variants. If they make intrinsically better poetry than texts *A-C*, then we might want to think that *D* reflects, in these instances, the original poem. As the last table shows, it is unique in two instances, in lines 6 and 16. The first comparable couplet in *A* reads:

> And our great Mountains, above and below,
> Are often-times cover'd with Ice and with Snow.

For "Ice" (present in *A-C*), *D* substitutes "frost." "Frost" is inferior for three reasons: first, because the New England mountains in winter are covered with ice, not frost; second, because "ice," not "frost," naturally complements "snow"; and third, because ice, being more severe than frost, better suits the spirit of the poem.

Therefore I reject "frost" as an authentic descendant of the original poem. Nevertheless, the word "frost" does, I believe, tend to confirm that *D* text is authentic. I reason that no would-be "improver" of the poem would change "ice" to "frost." I suspect that the change could only be made by mistake during an oral recitation. The other unique reading occurs in the following couplet (*A* text):

> While it is growing much Spoil there is made
> By Birds and by Squirrels that pluck up the Blade;

For "that" *(A-C)*, *D* text has "who." I think that "who" is slightly inferior, although it is a possibility. At any rate, this choice tells us nothing about *D* text's possible authenticity.

Returning to the complete table of *B-D* substantive variants and examining *D* text's remaining five (2, 4, 29, 34[1], and 38) unique variants (we have just discussed the three [6, 16, and 46] where comparable lines exist in *A* text), I judge that *D* text is about as good a choice as *B-C* in lines 4 and 29, but that it is slightly worse in lines 2, 34(1), and 38. In line 2, the choice of "does" instead of "doth" or "do" is ungrammatical, uncolloquial, and awkward. In lines 34(1) and 38 the singular, generalized form "pumpkin" instead of "pumkins" is again uncolloquial and in the latter line clashes with the normal plurals of "parsnips and walnut-tree chips."

Finally, *D* text does not seem to be quite as good a text as *B* or *C*. But that very fact supports the conclusion that it has some claims to authenticity, for the same old lady responsible for the other two texts evidently recited this text two years later, when she was 94 years old; and only the most inept bungler would have conflated *B* and *C* texts and then made those changes for the worse to produce *D* text. I believe that all three very similar texts were taken down from the same informant at different times. Since I will later chart the genealogy of the poem, it may be helpful to conclude this section with the following simple stemma:

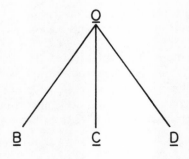

3. Other Texts

Three additional texts have been considered authentic. However, all three are extremely similar to *C* text and derive from it. To prove this, I provide the following table of substantive variants.

C = *Massachusetts Magazine* 3 (1791): 52–53.
E = Farmer and Moore, *Collections* 3 (1824): 230–31.
F = Alonzo Lewis, *History of Lynn* (1829), 35.
G = Massachusetts Historical Society *Collections*, 3d ser., 7 (1838): 29–30.

Substantive Variants Among C, E-G

1–2	[lacking in *E-F*]	
9	any's *C, E, G*	any is *F*
15	when *C, E, G*	while *F*
18	often *C, F, G*	after *E*
19	garments *C, G*	old garments *E, F*
28	pumpkins and turnips and fish *C, E, F*	turnips as much as we wish *G*
29	is there *C, E, G*	if there's *F*
30	repair *C, E, G*	haste *F*
31	Instead *C, E, G*	'Stead *F*
40	boiling *C, F, G*	a boiling *E*
43	But *C, E, G*	Then *F*

John Farmer and Jacob Bailey Moore printed the song in their *Collections, Historical and Miscellaneous: and Monthly Literary Journal* 3 (1824): 230–31 (*E* text). They entitled it "FOREFATHERS' SONG" and added the following prefatory headnote within brackets: "[Composed about the year 1630, taken *memoriter* in 1791, from the lips of an old lady, at the advanced age of 92]." The title and prefatory note are obviously from *C* text, except that Farmer and Moore have assumed that the date of publication of *C* text (1791) was identical with the time that the "old lady" recited the text. The only footnote, "Clout signifies patching," is taken from *C* text. The poem is printed in numbered octaves, with an italicized explanation after the fourth line of the fifth octave, *"(Four lines wanting)."* The arrangement of stanzas and the note evidently follow *C* text. As the above table testifies, *E* text differs from *C* in four substantives (1–2, 18, 19, and 40). In line 18 "after" for "often" is evidently an error, perhaps resulting from the printer's misreading the manuscript. The changes in lines 19 and 40 add unnecessary words, and the omission of lines 1–2 evidently arises because *C* text printed the couplet above the title as a prefatory epigraph, and so Farmer and Moore thought it not part of the poem. I conclude that *E* text is copied from *C* and that it may therefore be dismissed from further consideration.

The text in Alonzo Lewis, *History of Lynn* (Boston: Eastburn,

1829), 35, is much more interesting, and my friend Professor Harold Jantz once thought it had some claim to authenticity and so used it in his reconstruction of the original text.[16] Lewis includes practically no editorial matter. The *History of Lynn* is arranged by annals, with the poem appearing under "1630." The one sentence of prefatory matter reads: "The following song, which appears to have been written about this time, exhibits some of the peculiar customs and modes of thinking among the early settlers." (In later editions, Lewis replaced the word "song" with "ballad.") Lewis printed the poem in quatrains in the first edition; and, like Farmer and Moore (*E* text), he omitted the first two lines. In the second edition of the *History of Lynn* (Boston: S. N. Dickinson, 1844), 71–72, Lewis printed the poem in octaves, and added a quatrain (which he obviously composed) to complete stanza five, where, of course, both *C* text and *E* text say that four lines are missing. An examination of the four editions of the *History of Lynn* proves that Lewis, who was a poet as well as a historian, tampered with the poem. Here follows a list of Lewis's editions:

F^1 = *History of Lynn* (1829), p. 35.

F^2 = *History of Lynn, including Nahant* (1844), pp. 71–72.

F^3 = *History of Lynn, Essex County, Massachusetts* (1865), pp. 133–34.

F^4 = *History of Lynn, Essex County, Massachusetts* (1890), pp. 133–34.

In F^3 and F^4, the poem is again printed in quatrains and the added quatrain of F^2 is omitted. Here are the substantive variants in F^{1-4}:

11	But when F^1, F^2	And when F^3, F^4
30	there we catch fish F^1	take what we wish F^2, F^3, F^4
38–39	[Between these lines, F^2, in order to make six complete octaves, adds within brackets:]	
	[Stead of brandy and whiskey and cider and gin,	
	We have liquor which all may partake without sin;	
	Our springs of fresh water are excellent cheer,	
	And fill up the places of porter and beer.]	
44	will F^1	shall F^2, F^3, F^4

I suspect that Lewis's source was *E* text, for he not only followed it in omitting the first two lines, but he also added its unnecessary word "old" in line 19. If he did not know *C* text, he showed good judgment in correcting *E* text's "after" (18) back to "often" and in rejecting the unnecessary letter "a" (40). But these differences from *E* text make me think that Lewis (who, as a good local historian, would be familiar with the old *Massachusetts Magazine*) probably compared his copy of *E* text with *C* before producing his own version. Further, he belonged to the Massachusetts Historical Society, and when it published *G* text in 1838, he must have seen it.[17] I think *G* text, where line 28 concludes "turnips as much as we wish," inspired Lewis's change in line 30 of his second and following editions to "take what we wish." Of his six unique differences, two (9 and 31) merely involve contractions. One, replacing "when" by "while" (15), is a decided improvement, for "when" implies a specific time and "while" implies duration or process. Only this substantive variant might imply that *F* text has some claim to authority, for *B-D* texts all have "when," but *A* text has the superior "while." But I believe that in this one case, Lewis merely showed excellent judgment in making the change—and that his excellent judgment agreed with that of the original composer. Another change, substituting "if there's" (29) for "is there," tries to improve a vapid expression (texts *B-D* all differ). Lewis probably substituted "haste" for "repair" (30) partly for an anachronistic reason (the old meaning of the verb *repair*, to go, was becoming uncommon), partly because he preferred the more active verb (although its connotation of necessary swiftness is unwarranted by the context), and partly because he preferred a single, accented syllable for the meter. The final change (43), substituting "Then" for "But," seems to me clearly inferior. Perhaps Lewis was influenced by the word "Now" beginning the penultimate stanza, and believed "Then" would be a natural sequence to begin the final stanza. "But" seems better to me because it emphasizes the contrast between the traitors' leaving New England and the emigrants' arriving. I should also point out that Lewis's change, in the second and following editions, of the word "will" to "shall" (44) again shows excellent judgment—and it agrees with both *A* and *D* texts. Nevertheless, Lewis's text must stem from *C* and *E* texts; it was changed from one edition to another in stanzaic form as well as within the text itself; and the later editions were evidently influenced by *G* text. I conclude that his text is without authority.

The last text that we should consider (it has frequently been the source for later reprintings) appeared in the *Collections of the Massachusetts Historical Society*, 3d ser., 7 (1838): 29–30 (*G* text). It is entitled "OUR FOREFATHER'S SONG" and contains the following prefatory comment within brackets: "[Composed about the year 1630, author unknown; *taken memoriter, in* 1785, *from the lips of an old Lady, at the advanced period of* 96. *There is visibly a break in the sense, commencing at the 5th line of the 5th verse:* and, through the failure of memory, four lines have been lost at the latter part of the 5th stanza.]" The one footnote is keyed to line 22: "Clout signifies patching." The poem is printed in octaves, with the first two lines as a prefatory couplet and with asterisks filling out the last four lines of the fifth stanza. The prefatory material is generally copied from *C* text, even using the same italicization and other accidentals. And the only footnote uses the exact words of *C* text. Within *G* text itself, there is only one substantive difference (28, "Turnips as much as we wish" for *C* text's "pumpkins and turnips and fish"). Moreover *G* text is identical with *C* in all accidentals, except for capitalizing "Lord" in line 43. The conclusion is inescapable. *G* text is derived from *C* text and has no authority.

G text does, however, present an interesting complication, for it says that the song was supposedly written down "*in* 1785" and gives the old lady's age as 96 rather than 92 (*C* text). (In *D* text, her age was given as 94 in 1767; and in *B* text, as 92, when she "lately" "recollected and repeated" the song.) Although one might suspect that *G* text was copied from some unknown text printed in 1785 (which, in turn, was the source of *C* text), I consider this unlikely, partly because of the change in the old lady's age to 96 and partly because of the one substantive difference. Instead, I suspect that these changes reflect the tamperings of an editor.

I conclude that the only known texts that have any claim to authority are *A-D*. The following stemma represents my hypothesis of the relationship of texts *A-C* to the original.

Ur	=	the original text
O	=	the old lady
A	=	*Father Abraham's Speech*, (Boston, 1758)
B	=	*Massachusetts Spy*, 3 February 1774, 4/1
C	=	*Massachusetts Magazine* 3 (January 1791): 52–53
D	=	*Old Colony Memorial*, 18 May 1822, 1/4–2/1
E	=	Farmer and Moore, *Collections* 3 (1824): 230–31
F	=	Alonzo Lewis, *History of Lynn* (1829), 35
G	=	*Collections of the Massachusetts Historical Society*, 3d ser., 7 (1838): 29–30
F²	=	Lewis, *History of Lynn* (1844)
F³	=	Lewis, *History of Lynn* (1865)
F⁴	=	Lewis, *History of Lynn* (1890)

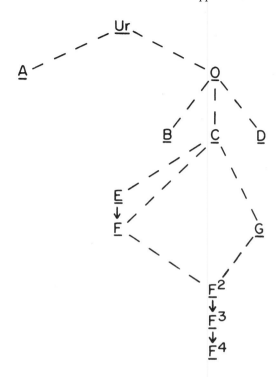

4. Rationale for Reconstruction

Several objections can be raised against attempting to reconstruct the original song. First, the result will not be authentic: the resulting hypothetical Ur-text will bastardize the two quite different versions of "New England's Annoyances" that have descended to us. Second, the hypothetical reconstruction may not have the unity of either of the two traditional songs. Third, we cannot be sure that some stanzas in the two different texts were not added by a transmitter of the text. And fourth, like previous well-meaning editors who distorted the song's structure in an attempt to make sense of what they found in their sources, we may make the same error. In answering these objections, I must stress that I do not claim the reconstruction is a faithful approximation of the original. All that I claim is that the result will be more complete and closer to the original than either traditional version.

The only authentic texts are *A-D*, and they are the texts of an anonymous folk song. The hypothetical reconstruction *is* hypothetical. Studies of typical changes made in the process of oral transmission show that folk songs tend to degenerate as various singers forget words, lines, or stanzas of the original and as singers forget the original tunes.[18] In such cases, singers sometimes substitute other words, suggested by the song's previous phrases or by phrases or even stanzas from other songs. Therefore, I have supposed that as we make the best possible choices among the basic texts, we approach the original song. It could be that a singer actually improved the song during the course of its transmission. Or it is possible that, in choosing what seems to be the best from several possibilities, I will combine mistakes made by different singers. But both these possibilities are unlikely, for the two basic texts, *A* and the *B-D* group (the latter, evidently, all from the same source) are quite similar in those lines that the two songs have in common. Nevertheless, the variants within the *B-D* group testify that even an individual singer did remember the song differently on different occasions. The argument for reconstructing the hypothetical original must finally depend upon the individual details for its justification. Therefore, I will give all the evidence as well as all the most compelling reasons for every choice as I reconstruct the hypothetical original.

One can be relatively sure that *A* text and the *B-D* group contain only lines originally present in the song. No one, I trust, doubts that the twenty-six lines shared by the two texts were part of the original. Twenty-two additional lines (ten from *A* and twelve from *B-D*) deal with the same subjects as the lines the two share. Moreover, these twenty-two lines provide either openings, closings, or transitions for the lines that the two versions have in common. I do not believe that anyone could doubt that they belong to the original. Eight more lines, unique to the *B-D* group, are on New England food. They immediately precede the lines on New England drink in the *B-D* texts and are a natural subject to follow the earlier stanzas (shared by both texts) on the difficulties of raising crops. Logically, they should have been—and I believe were—part of the original. That leaves only eight lines, all from *A* text, four on New England's lack of a medium of exchange (currency), and four on New England's religion. Since New England currency as a subject does not survive in any seventeenth-century song, I think it unlikely to suppose that it was borrowed from another song. And although several other seventeenth-century songs deal with New England's religion, all of the others are satirical; this is not. These eight lines are undoubtedly examples of "New England's Annoyances," possess the same style and spirit as the rest of the poem, and represent especially pressing problems at the time the original song was composed (c. 1643).

The reconstruction is a more unified composition than either *A* or the *B-D* group alone. Only the *B-D* group contains the title and the natural opening of the song—the first quatrain, which announces the general subject. But only *A* text provides the transition from the general subject to the first major topic (the severity of New England winters). The *B-D* group is simply incomplete without this couplet. Then the two texts share a couplet (*A* 3-4 = *B-D* 5-6); but only the *B-D* group contains the logically sequential second quatrain on the topic of New England's cold winters (*B-D* 7-10). And so it goes throughout the poem. Two difficulties (discussed below) in sequence and transition will remain after combining these two basic texts, but the probable explanation for these possible lacunae is either that some quatrains of the original song are not present in the two basic texts or that the original author saw no need for an absolutely logical development.

As I have pointed out, if the original tune was "Derry Down," then the original stanzaic structure must have been the quatrain. Although one could wish that the *B-D* groups of texts named the tune, the anapestic tetrameter line calls for the "Derry Down" melody.[19] Even without the authority of *A* text, a nineteenth-century authority hypothesized that "Derry Down" was the tune.[20] The evidence of *A* text confirms the stanzaic arrangement and the melody.

5. *Alternatives among the* B-D *Texts*

My first step in reconstructing a hypothetical Ur-text is to select the best reading among the versions within the *B-D* group. I cite *B* text and briefly discuss the choices (see the table *Substantive Variants, B-D,* p. 100 above).

1. NEW-England's annoyances you that would know them
2. Pray ponder these verses which briefly do show them;

In line 2, *C* text has "doth" and *D* has "does." I prefer "doth" because Edward Johnson characteristically uses "doth" rather than "do." "Does" in *D* is ungrammatical and awkward.

3. The place where we live is a wilderness wood,
4. Where grass is much wanting that's fruitful and good:

In line 4, I reject "wanted" (D) in favor of "wanting" (B and C) because the former adds a possible personal element into what is otherwise primarily a straightforward, impersonal description of unpleasant reality.

>   5. Our mountains and hills and valleys below
>   6. Being commonly cover'd with ice and with snow,

In line 5, C text adds "our" (before "valleys"), which is unnecessary and redundant (it was evidently added to regularize the meter). And in line 6, I reject "frost" (D) in favor of the more severe and accurate "ice" (B and C) which is confirmed by A text.

>   7. And when the north-wester with violence blows
>   8. Then every man pulls his cap over his nose;

I prefer "north-wester" (B) to "northwest wind" (C) and (D). The former is shorter and more effective: a "north-wester" suggests a full-scale storm whereas a "northwest wind" could be comparatively mild. Besides, "north-wester" better suits the meter.

>   9. But if any are so hardy and will it withstand,
>   10. He forfeits a finger, a foot or a hand.

In line 9, I prefer "any's" (C) to "any are" (B) and (D) partly because it better suits the meter, partly because it is more colloquial (thus complementing the tone), and partly because the grammar is better.

Of the six substantive differences in the first ten lines, I find that I prefer B text in four instances and C text in two. Evidently B text is generally a slightly better text (and thus, I believe, a text slightly closer to the original) than either C or D.

>   11. When the spring opens we then take the hoe
>   12. And make the ground ready to plant and to sow;

In line 11, I prefer "When" (B and D) to "But when" (C), even though A has "And when." Although the line begins a new stanza and a new topic, the conjunction "But" (or "And") is unnecessary. I suspect that both A and C texts have been influenced by the formulaic tendency common in oral transmission. The next couplet (lines 13–14) is the same in all these texts.

15. And when it is growing, some spoil there is made,
16. By birds and by squirrels that pluck up the blade,

In line 16, I reject "who" *(D)* in favor of "that" *(B and C)*, confirmed by *A* and obviously superior.

17. Even when it is grown to full corn in the ear,
18. It is often destroyed by racoons and deer.

In line 17, I prefer "Even when" *(B and D)* to "And when" *(C)*, although "And when" is confirmed by *A* text. "Even" is a good example of diction that would tend to be replaced in oral transmission by the simpler, formulaic "and." "Even" seems superior because of the more interesting meter and especially because it emphasizes the poem's wry humor. Further on in line 17, I prefer "grown" *(B and D)* to "come" *(C)*, partly because *A* confirms "grown." The attraction of "come" depends upon its stronger connotations of fulfillment and its alliteration with "corn." On the other hand, "grow" echoes "growing" *(A 9)* and thereby adds to the verbal unity of the song. And in line 18, since I prefer the reading in *A* text to the variations within *C-D*, I will not attempt to choose among them.

The next quatrain (lines 19–22) is identical in the three texts.

23. Our cloaths we brought with us are often much torn,
24. They need to be clouted before they are worn;

In line 23, I reject "often much" *(B)* in favor of "apt to be" *(C and D)*, confirmed by *A* text. The couplet stresses that clothes must be patched because they have been torn by frequent wear in the wilderness. "Apt to be" emphasizes that the clothes have already been torn, whereas "often much" implies that the clothes are presently being torn and worn out and it even rather awkwardly suggests that the clothes were already torn at the time they were brought over. The point, of course, is that just enough time has passed since the immigrants arrived in America so that their clothes are "apt to be torn." In line 24, "before" *(B)* confirmed by *A*, is clearly superior to "soon after" *(C and D)*. Further along in line 24, "they are" *(B and D)* seems metrically preferable to "They're" *(C)*.

27. If flesh meat be wanting to fill up our dish,
28. We have carrets and pumpkins and turnips and fish;

In line 27, "flesh" *(B* and *D)* makes good sense, whereas "fresh" *(C)* may be anachronistic (as I pointed out above) and it weakens the couplet's meaning.

> 29. And when we have a mind for a delicate dish,
> 30. We repair to the *clam-bank* and there we catch fish.

In line 29, the three different readings—"when we have" *(B)*, "is there a" *(C)*, and "if we have" *(D)*—all seem reasonably good, but I prefer *B* partly because *B* text is generally more reliable, partly because "is there a" *(C)* seems slightly awkward, partly because the "if" *(D)* does not seem as normal to human realities as "when" *(B)*, and partly because I suspect that "if" is memorial, being influenced by the initial "If" of line 27. In line 30, I prefer "clam banks" *(C)* to "clam-bank" *(B* and *D)*, because the former is more colloquial and more accurate. The singular "clam-bank" suggests that there was only one "clam-bank" or only one place (called the clam bank) to go for shellfish and fish.

> 33. We have pumkin at morning, and pumkin at noon.
> 34. If it was not for pumkins we would be *undoon*.

In line 33, I prefer the generic singular of "pumkin" *(B* and *D)* to the plural "pumkins" *(C)*, although here the distinction may be simply a matter of taste. But in line 34, I prefer the plural "pumkins" to the generic singular "pumkin" *(D)*, for here the plural is striking and accurate.

After another couplet (35–36) with no substantive variants, we have:

> 37. For *we* can make liquor to sweeten our lips,
> 38. Of pumkins and parsnips and walnut-tree chips.

In line 38 as in line 34, *D* text introduces a generic singular ("pumkin") where the realistic plural "pumkins" *(B* and *C)* is more suitable; besides, the plural complements the line's other two plural nouns.

> 39. Now while some are going let others be coming,
> 40. For while liquor is boiling it must have a scumming,

In line 40, I reject the contraction "liquor's" *(C)* in favor of "liquor is" *(B* and *D)* partly because the meter is more regular, partly because "liquor's" is not as clear in meaning as "liquor is," and partly because the separate words emphasize the proverbial quality of the line.

> 41. But we will not blame them, for birds of a feather,
> 42. By seeking their fellows are flocking together.

In line 41, I slightly prefer "we" *(B)* to "I" *(C* and *D)*, even though "I" is confirmed by *A.* The first person plural is generally used throughout the poem and seems more suitable than the personal pronoun for the tone and themes of the song. I recognize, however, that the change in person could be argued to be more dramatic and forceful—and therefore preferable.

> 43. But you who the Lord intends hither to bring,
> 44. Forsake not the honey for fear of the sting,

In line 43, I reject "whom" *(C)* in favor of "who" *(B* and *D)*, for the introduction of the correct objective case into a colloquial poem clashes with the tone. I believe that it anachronistically reflects late-eighteenth-century tastes.

> 45. But bring both a quiet and contented mind
> 46. And all needful blessings you surely will find.

And in the last line, I prefer "shall" *(C)* to "will" *(B* and *D)*, partly because *A* concurs with *C*, partly because of the alliteration with "surely," and partly because of the greater emphasis and definiteness of "shall."

In 17 instances (lines 4, 5, 6, 7, 11, 17 [twice], 24 [twice], 27, 29, 33, 34, 38, 40, 41, and 43), I have selected *B* text as preferable; in one case (line 18), I prefer not to make a decision because the comparable line in *A* is different and, I believe, superior; and in six instances I have chosen either *C* or *D* texts as preferable. Of these five emendations to *B* text, one choice (in line 2) is influenced by my knowledge of the supposed author's usual practice; two (23 and 46) are confirmed by *A;* and two (9 and 30) are chosen entirely on their own intrinsic merits. Therefore, the text of *B* that I use in reconstructing the hypothetical Ur-text has been emended in the following five substantives:

Adopted Emendation	Rejected
2. doth *C*	do *B*, does *D*
9. any's *C*	any are *B*, *D*
23. apt to be *C*, *D*	often much *B*
30. clam banks *C*	clam-bank *B*, *D*
46. shall *D*	will *B*, *C*

6. *Alternatives between* A *and* B *Texts*

I now compare the thirteen couplets that *A* and *B* texts have in common, attempting to choose the better version for the reconstructed, hypothetical Ur-text. My assumption in choosing the intrinsically better version is that the original song has been corrupted in the process of oral transmission by faulty memory, resulting in formulaic and memorial substitutions and in the corruptions of popular etymology. Although we will find that *B* text (as emended in five instances from *C* and/or *D* texts) is generally superior to *A*, this does not mean the poem has been improved during the process of oral transmission (even though *B* was first printed sixteen years later than *A*). The *B-D* group is not descended from *A* but from an entirely different line of oral transmission, since each text has unique couplets and quatrains evidently belonging to the original.

Wherever I have adopted a couplet for the reconstructed text entirely from one version, the identifying sigla (*A* or *B*) is prefaced by an asterisk. Where I have combined the two, I have written out the reconstruction after the discussion.

> 1) *A*   3–4: And our great Mountains, above and below,
>   Are often-times cover'd with Ice and with Snow.
>   **B*   5–6: Our mountains and hills and valleys below
>   Being commonly cover'd with ice and with snow,

The first line of *A* text is metrically more interesting but wordy; and the last part of the line ("above and below") is less clear than *B*. In the second line, I prefer "Being" *(B)* to "Are" *(A)* because "Being" makes this couplet comment on and explain the previous couplet (unique to *A* text), where the ground is said to be "frozen as hard as a stone" for three months. Although "Are" *(A)* would be preferable if we consider this couplet alone, "Are" tends to make this couplet repetitious when the quatrain is considered as a whole. And since "commonly" *(B)* expresses more frequency than "often-times"

(A), I prefer *B* because it better suits the reality and the poem's wry humor.

    2) *A*   5–6: And when the Ground opens we then take a Hoe,
                       And make the Ground ready to plant and to sow;
       B 11–12: When the spring opens we then take the hoe
                       And make the ground ready to plant and to sow;

The only substantive differences between these two couplets occur in the first line. Without considering the contexts, one might find *B* superior because "spring opens" has so many interesting poetic possibilities, whereas "ground opens" *(A)* is limited to the thawing of the frozen ground. Also, it might seem that "ground" is an awkward repetition and possibly a memorial anticipation of "ground" in the following line. But *B* has lost an earlier couplet that introduced the topic of the severity of New England winters: "From the End of *November* till three Months are gone, / The Ground is all frozen as hard as a Stone" *(A* 1–2*)*. Therefore, "ground opens" *(A)*, which introduces the next topic (crops) of the poem, serves as a refrain, as a unifying device, and as a structural key ("ground . . . frozen" introduced one topic; eight lines later, "ground opens" introduces the next). Although "Ground" thus provides a superior reconstruction to the Ur-text, I should note that without the prior lines that are unique to *A*, *B* text ("spring") would be superior. Here is evidence of an improvement (given the loss of the previous lines) during oral transmission. Except for the key difference between "ground" *(A)* and "spring" *(B)*, I think that *B* text is superior. In *A* text, the introductory conjunction "And" is unnecessary and probably formulaic. Either "a Hoe" *(A)* or "the hoe" *(B)* contains a possible awkwardness, for both suggest that several people pick up one hoe ("we then take a Hoe"). Either choice may be justified, but I think "the hoe" *(B)* is less liable to objection. Therefore I prefer *B* text, only substituting "Ground" for "spring":

          When the Ground opens we then take the hoe
          And make the ground ready to plant and to sow;

    3) *A*   7–8: But Corn being planted, and Seed being sown,
                     The Worms eat much of it before it is grown.

*B 13–14: Our corn being planted and seed being sown,
            The worms destroy much before it is grown;

"But" in *A* seems like an awkward repetition of "But" in the previous couplet. I prefer "destroy much" *(B)* to "eat much of it" *(A)*
because the former is shorter and because the latter awkwardly
repeats "it," is not as accurate, and is metrically poor.

4) *A*   9–10: While it is a growing much Spoil there is made
                 By Birds and by Squirrels that pluck up the Blade;
    B 15–16: And when it is growing, some spoil there is made,
                 By birds and by squirrels that pluck up the blade,

"A growing" *(A)* seems padded and too colloquial. "Some" *(B)*
seems more accurate than "much" *(A)*, which may be a verbal echo
of "much" in *A* 8; but the exaggerated ironic humor of "much"
better suits the general tone of the poem. "While" *(A)* is better than
"when" *(B)*, because growing is a process and "while" emphasizes
process, whereas "when" indicates a particular time. "And when"
(B) occurs three more times in the poem (*B* 7; *A* 5 = *B* 11; *A* 11 = *B*
17): this incremental repetition may be the work of the original
poet, but it is more likely a memorial formula introduced in oral
transmission. "While" *(A)* also foreshadows the penultimate quatrain of the song and helps to make the ending seem appropriate.
The second line is the same in both texts. My reconstruction is:

            While it is growing much spoil there is made,
            By birds and by squirrels that pluck up the blade;

5) *A* 11–12: And when it is grown to full Corn in the Ear,
                 It's apt to be spoil'd by Hog, Racoon, and Deer.
    B 17–18: Even when it is grown to full corn in the ear,
                 It is often destroyed by racoons and deer.

In the first line, "Even" is better than "And" because it emphasizes
the wry humor. "Even" is also the kind of diction that would, I
suspect, tend to be replaced in oral tradition by the simple formulaic "And." In the second line, the metrical complexity of *A* compared to *B* suggests that *A* is closer to the original. I believe that, in
the process of oral transmission, *A* could easily be changed to *B*,
but it seems unlikely that the easy rhythm of *B* would become the

difficult (but more interesting) meter of *A*. In addition, in early-seventeenth-century New England, hogs commonly ran free and were a major problem to crops, but after the early years of each new settlement, they were usually fenced in.[21] I suspect that the changing conditions partially account for *B* text. Although "spoil'd" *(A)* may simply echo "Spoil" *(A 9)*, the common seventeenth-century meaning of *spoil* was "to strip or despoil" *(OED*, I, 1), a more graphic and accurate account of the destruction of corn by raccoon and deer (and hogs) than "destroy" *(B)*. I suggest the following reconstruction:

> Even when it is grown to full corn in the ear,
> It's apt to be spoil'd by hog, racoon, and deer.

6)   *A* 17–18: And now our Apparel begins to grow thin,
             And Wool is much wanted to card and to spin.
  *B 19–20: And now our garments begin to grow thin,
             And wool is much wanted to card and to spin;

I prefer "garments" *(B)* to "Apparel" *(A)* because the lower level of diction is more in keeping with the poem's tone, because the "g" in "garments" alliterates with "begin" and "grow," and because "begin" makes a perfect internal rhyme with "thin" (the selection of "Apparel" necessitates the imperfect rhyme "begins"). Besides, the cumulative effect of the repetition of "garments" (which recurs twice in the next couplet) adds to the poem's humor.

7)   *A* 19–20: If we get a Garment to cover without,
             Our innermost Garment is Clout upon Clout.
   B 21–22: If we can get a garment to cover without,
             Our other in-garments are clout upon clout;

Although "can" in the first line is redundant, it emphasizes the probability that the New Englanders may not be able to get an overcoat. It also varies the meter. Therefore I prefer *B*'s first line. But *B*'s second line does not make good sense: "other in-garments" suggests that the song has already listed some "in-garments." The line bothered Samuel Eliot Morison (he did not know *A* text), who suggested that "in-garments" referred to clothing worn indoors.[22] *A* text has a nice antithesis, contrasting the outer garment to the "innermost" one. It is also more humorous, partly because the "innermost" garment would be next to the sexual organs. There-fore, I prefer A's second line. My reconstruction is:

> If we can get a Garment to cover without,
> Our innermost Garment is Clout upon Clout.

8)   A 21–22: Our Cloth it is *boughten*, it's apt to be torn,
                    It need to be clouted before it is worn.
   *B 23–24 Our clothes we brought with us are apt to be torn,
                    They need to be clouted before they are worn;

A text has a lower level of grammatical usage than the rest of the poem. And B is clearer. The first line of A does not make good sense: "bought" cloth is not "apt to be torn," unlike clothes "brought" over from England several years ago.

9) *A 23–24: For clouting our Garments does injure us Nothing:
                 Clouts double are warmer than single whole Cloathing.
   B 25–26: But clouting our garments they hinder us nothing,
                 Clouts double are warmer than single whole cloathing.

The only substantive differences are in the first line, where "For" seems slightly preferable to "But" *(B)* and where "does injure" *(A)* makes better sense than "they hinder" *(B);* therefore, I prefer A.

10) A 37–38 But while such are going, let others be coming.
                 Whilst Liquors are boiling, they should have a Scumming:
   *B 39–40: Now while some are going let others be coming,
                 For while liquor is boiling it must have a scumming,

"But while such" *(A)* and "Now while some" *(B)* leave little to choose between. "Some" *(B)* may be a better antithesis with "others" *(A and B)* than "such" *(A);* and "such" may be simply a memorial echo of the same word in A 33. Conversely, "such" has connotations of contemptuousness and may therefore be more suit-able. This seems to be an instance where the change (whichever text was changed) made during oral transmission reveals some judg-ment, since "but" complements "such" (emphasizing the contemp-tuous connotations of the latter word), while "Now" *(B)* comple-ments "some" (prefiguring the see-saw relationship of "some" and "others"). In the second line, B text is clearly superior.

11) *A* 39–40: And I cannot blame'em, since *Birds of a Feather*
              Are chusing their Fellows by flocking together.
   *B 41–42: But we will not blame them, for birds of a feather,
              By seeking their fellows are flocking together.

As I pointed out in discussing the *B–D* variants, I believe that "we" *(B)* is more suitable to the general tone and theme of the poem. "Will not" *(B)* seems better than "cannot" *(A)*, since the author obviously does blame the malcontents who returned to England. And "seeking" *(B)* seems preferable to "chusing" partially because it implies more effort. Also, in the first line, "for" seems slightly better than "since" because of the alliteration (feather, fellows, flocking).

12) *A* 41–42: But you that the LORD intends hither to bring,
              Forsake not your Honey *for Fear of a* Sting;
   *B 43–44: But you who the LORD intends hither to bring,
              Forsake not the honey for fear of the sting,

I suspect that the original was "who" and that it was changed to "that" in the process of oral transmission—but this is a toss-up. In the second line, the personal note "your Honey" seems out of place (cf. *B*'s "the honey") in the religious context of the couplet. On the whole, I prefer *B*.

13) *A* 43–44: But bring both a quiet and contented Mind,
              And all *needful* Blessings you surely shall find.
   B 45–46: But bring both a quiet and contented mind
              And all needful blessings you surely shall find.

Of the thirteen couplets that *A* and *B* texts have in common, only this final one has no substantive differences, although *B* text has been emended from *D* text.

7. The Song's Structure

A final consideration before reconstructing the hypothetical Ur-text concerns the sequence within the poem. Eleven couplets are unique to *A*, and ten couplets are unique to *B*. We have an excellent guide to the original order of the poem, for both *A* and *B* texts retain the same sequence for all lines that they share:

A (1758)		B (1774)	Subject
3–4	=	5–6	cold climate
5–12	=	11–18	crops
17–24	=	19–26	clothing
37–44	=	39–46	concluding appeal

In addition to the evidence supplied by the same sequence in two versions, the meaning suggests that this sequence is correct, for the issues tend to become more serious as the poem progresses, and the ending (present in both texts) makes the point toward which the entire poem builds. And as I showed (chapter 1), the topics and their sequence are similar to the promotion tract's usual organization. I conclude that the song's sequence—at least for the lines common to both A and B texts—is correct. Since the two versions are in the correct sequence for the lines that they share, the lines unique to each version are probably also in the proper order. Therefore, in adding the twenty-one unique couplets, I will attempt to retain the present sequence of both poems—so long as this order is not inconsistent with a logical and artful progression.

The first couplet of B text introduces the general subject of the poem and should, I am sure, open the poem. This couplet provided the title for the poem—a common practice, especially in songs—and is obviously part of the poem, for it is echoed (A 33) near the conclusion:

[1]
NEW-England's annoyances you that would know them
Pray ponder these verses which briefly doth show them:

(B 1–2)

The second couplet of B text consists of generalized description and should precede the account of New England's cold winters (which opens A and which obviously belongs with the two quatrains on that subject):

The place where we live is a wilderness wood,
Where grass is much wanting that's fruitful and good:

(B 3–4)

These four lines form the opening quatrain, introducing the subject and beginning the catalogue of complaints.

The first specific subject for sustained complaint in both versions is the long, cold New England winter. The unique lines in *A* introduce this topic:

[2]
FROM the End of *November* till three Months are gone,   5
The Ground is all frozen as hard as a Stone,

(*A* 1–2)

The next couplet, present in both texts, is:

Our mountains and hills and valleys below
Being commonly cover'd with ice and with snow,

(no. 1, in section 6, above)

Text *B* then has a unique quatrain on cold weather. Because this quatrain continues the former subject, it belongs before the description of spring and the raising of crops common to both texts:

[3]
And when the north-wester with violence blows
Then every man pulls his cap over his nose;   10
But if any's so hardy and will it withstand,
He forfeits a finger, a foot or a hand.

(*B* 7–10)

Next, both texts contain eight lines on the raising of corn, beginning with a transition from the former topic:

[4]
When the Ground opens we then take the hoe
And make the ground ready to plant and to sow;
Our corn being planted and seed being sown,   15
The worms destroy much before it is grown;

[5]
While it is growing much spoil there is made,
By birds and by squirrels that pluck up the blade;
Even when it is grown to full corn in the ear,
It's apt to be spoil'd by hog, racoon, and deer.   20

(nos. 2, 3, 4, and 5, above)

A text now includes a stanza on the scarcity of currency and the consequent necessity for bartering and swapping. There is no obvious connection between the previous stanzas and the quatrain on currency. It is not a commonplace stanza (i.e., one found in various folk songs, added by the singer when he wants to lengthen out, or has forgotten, a stanza), for it was indubitably a New England annoyance. There are two possibilities for the position of the currency stanza. First, it can remain where it is in the sequence of *A* text (i.e., as stanza 6 in the reconstructed text). The author's attitude suggests that the currency problem is not terribly serious; it only makes "all our Dealings uncertain and strange." (After the colonies began issuing their own currencies, the problem became politically important.)[23] Moreover, this stanza does lead into the following two quatrains on clothing, because it concerns something that the colonists brought over from England. The clause "we brought with us" (22) is repeated in the first line of stanza 8 (29), thus binding stanzas 6 through 8 together. Further, it does not concern so serious a hardship as the next two stanzas (since clothes are a necessity). One might, however, argue that the poem's most artistic order would progress from a consideration of the necessities of life (climate, food, clothing, and drink) to the particular relations of New Englanders with one another (money and religion). In that case, the stanza on currency would follow those on clothing, food, and drink, and immediately precede the stanza on religion. (It would be stanza 12 in the combined version.) Of course, one might argue that the original poem has lost one or more stanzas (it may well have) and that, given the fragmentary nature of the surviving versions, it is impossible to tell with certainty where, in the poem, the stanza on currency belongs. But I think the most logical sequence demands that we place the quatrain here, where it will lead into the quatrains on clothing. Besides, I would need a good reason to displace the stanza from its present position in the sequence of *A* text.

[6]
Our Money's soon counted, for we have just none,
All that we brought with us is wasted and gone.
We buy and sell Nothing but upon Exchange,
Which makes all our Dealings uncertain and strange.

(*A* 13–16)

Both versions now contain two quatrains on clothing, which, like the currency, was also brought over from England:

[7]
And now our garments begin to grow thin,   25
And wool is much wanted to card and to spin;

If we can get a Garment to cover without,
Our innermost Garment is Clout upon Clout.

[8]
Our clothes we brought with us are apt to be torn,
They need to be clouted before they are worn;   30
For clouting our Garments does injure us Nothing:
Clouts double are warmer than single whole Cloathing.

(nos. 6, 7, 8, and 9, above)

At this point, *A* and *B* texts each have three unique stanzas. *A* has one on New England drink, one on religion, and one on malcontents who return to England. *B* text has two quatrains on New England food and one on drink. Since each text has a unique stanza on the same subject—drink—and since these two quatrains evidently belong together, the sequence of these six quatrains is suggested by the position of the stanzas on drink in *A* and *B* texts. First comes *B* text's two stanzas on food, then the stanzas on drink from *A* and *B* (I will examine their sequence below), then the two quatrains that follow in *B* text, the first on religion and the second on malcontents. This sequence makes excellent sense. The quatrain on malcontents clearly belongs just before the last two stanzas of the poem, which both texts have in common and which continue the subject of possible emigration from New England. And the unique stanza on religion (*A* text), which precedes the unique stanza on malcontents, deals with a more serious and important subject than any previous "annoyance." Therefore it should be the final "annoyance" in the song and should come just before the conclusion. The two quatrains on food and the two on drink clearly complement one another, not only because of the natural and commonplace association and sequence of these two topics, but also because each is introduced by a similar construction and by identical words ("If flesh meat be wanting" [33]; "If barly be wanting" [41]). Moreover, these clauses echo the earlier one on clothing ("And wool is much wanted" [26]), in stanza 7. Therefore we have a continuous series of interlocking and complementary phrases from the sixth quatrain ("we brought with us" [22 and 29] in stanzas 6 and 8) through stanza 12.

Here, then, are the two stanzas on food:

[9]
If flesh meat be wanting to fill up our dish,
We have carrets and pumkins and turnips and fish;
And when we have a mind for a delicate dish,   35
We repair to the *clam-banks* and there we catch fish.

[10]
Instead of pottage and puddings and custards and pies,
Our pumkins and parsnips are common supplies;
We have pumkin at morning, and pumkin at noon,
If it was not for pumkins we should be undoon.   40
                                                    (B 27–34)

Next come the two quatrains on drink. But in what order? I believe
that the unique *B* quatrain should come first. The drinks in *B* are
more acceptable than those in *A* (thus the wry humor increases); the
mention of pumpkins in *B* links this stanza with the two previous
ones on food; the opening in *B* echoes the opening (33) of the two
stanzas on food; the last couplet in *A* rounds off the lines on drink;
and the last couplet in *A* marks the turn in the song from a burlesque, dry humor to a serious tone. Thus the last couplet in *A*
leads into the serious quatrain on religion.

[11]
If barley be wanting to make into malt,
We must be contented, and think it no fault,
For *we* can make liquor to sweeten our lips,
Of pumkins and parsnips and walnut-tree chips.

                                                    (B 35–38)

[12]
And of our green Corn-Stalks we make our *best* Beer,   45
We put it in Barrels to drink all the Year:
Yet I am as healthy, I verily think,
Who make the Spring-Water my commonest Drink.

                                                    (A 25–28)

Then comes the unique stanza on religion, the last and most serious
complaint.

[13]
And we have a Cov'nant one with another,
Which makes a Division 'twixt Brother and Brother: 50
For some are rejected, and others *made* SAINTS,
Of those that are *equal* in Virtues and Wants.

                                                    (A 29–32)

The last unique quatrain concerns malcontents *(A)*. By repeating
the key word of the title and opening line, "Annoyance," it pre-
pares for the song's conclusion. And it leads into the penultimate
stanza.

[14]
For such like Annoyance we've many mad Fellows
Find Fault with our Apples before they are mellow;
And they are for ENGLAND, they will not stay here,   55
But *Meet with a Lion in shunning a Bear.*

(*A* 33–36)

Finally there are the two concluding stanzas (present in both texts), the first making a transition from the subject of malcontents ("some are going") to the concluding invitation.

[15]
Now while some are going let others be coming,
For while liquor is boiling it must have a scumming,
But we will not blame them, for birds of a feather,
By seeking their fellows are flocking together.   60

[16]
But you who the LORD intends hither to bring,
Forsake not the honey for fear of the sting,
But bring both a quiet and contented mind,
And all needful blessings you surely shall find.

(nos. 10, 11, 12, and 13, above)

Thus, the sequence of the poem should be, I believe, as follows:

Stanza	*Source*	*Topic*
1	*B* 1–4	general subject; little grass
2	*A* 1–2	the cold winters
	no. 1 = *B* 5–6; *A* 3–4	"
3	*B* 7–10	"
4	nos. 2–3 = *B* 11–14; *A* 5–8	difficulty of raising corn
5	nos. 4–5 = *B* 15–18; *A* 9–12	"
6	*A* 13–16	lack of currency
7	no. 6 = *B* 19–20; *A* 17–18	worn-out clothing
	no. 7 = *A* 19–20; *B* 21–22	"
8	no. 8 = *B* 23–24; *A* 21–22	"
	no. 9 = *A* 23–24; *B* 25–26	"
9	*B* 27–30	food-pumpkins
10	*B* 31–34	"
11	*B* 35–38	drink-water
12	*A* 25–28	"
13	*A* 29–32	religion
14	*A* 33–36	malcontents
15	nos. 10–11 *B* 39–42; *A* 37–40	"
16	nos. 12–13 *B* 43–46; *A* 41–44	closing invitation

From the opening through stanza 5 (concluding the two stanzas on the difficulties of raising corn), a logical sequence of thought is sustained, with natural transitions. Between stanzas 5 and 6 (on currency), a break in thought occurs, and a quatrain (or more) may be missing here. Since there are two stanzas each on New England winters, crops, clothing, food, drink, and malcontents, there may have been two on currency (and later in the poem, two on religion). Stanza 6, however, does seem to anticipate the following stanzas on clothing (both currency and clothes were brought over from England; the former is disappearing, and the latter, wearing out). Further, stanzas 6 through 12 contain verbal similarities (lines 22 and 29, and lines 26, 33, 41) that interlock and unify them. With the last couplet of stanza 12, the voice changes from first person plural to first person singular, the wry, boasting, humorous tone becomes serious, and the drinks change from various strange home brews to the ascetic water. All these changes lead naturally into the thirteenth stanza, on New England's religion. And the thirteenth through the sixteenth stanzas form a logical sequence. Thus, I conclude not only that all of the lines in the two separate folk songs belong to the original song, but also that if any stanzas of the original song are missing, they probably come after the fifth stanza.

Finally, I must repeat that although the reconstructed hypothetical Ur-text is more complete than either separate version, I do not claim it is a faithful text of the original poem. I believe it is a better poem than either separate version, for it is better unified, more interesting, and more complete. I suspect that the song was originally printed as a broadside, but unless a copy or reprint of the original turns up, the hypothetical reconstruction is probably as close to the original as we can come. It is pointless to preserve the idiosyncratic accidentals of either of the two main sources (A or B) of the hypothetical Ur-text, for both are from the oral tradition. The peculiarities of spelling, punctuation, capitalization, and italicization can only represent the whims of the transcribers or printers. And if I tried to maintain the accidentals faithfully, they would necessarily be a combination of the two styles (A and B), with B text influenced by two other styles (C and D). Therefore, I have not attempted to force a meaningless and impossible consistency upon the accidentals in my reconstruction but have normalized them. If a reader wants to see the original accidentals, he may find them faithfully followed (except for the identations beginning the quatrains of A and the octaves of B) in the reconstruction given in this section. The prologue contains my normalized reconstruction.

Notes

Chapter 1. Promotion Tracts and Satirical Ballads

1. Howard M. Jones discusses the varieties of promotion literature in "The Colonial Impulse: An Analysis of the 'Promotion' Literature of Colonization," *Proceedings of the American Philosophical Society* 90 (1946): 131–61. Hugh T. Lefler has described the "Promotional Literature of the Southern Colonies," *Journal of Southern History* 33 (1967): 3–25. And Louis B. Wright has examined several of promotion literature's major motifs: *Religion and Empire: The Alliance Between Piety and Commerce in English Expansion* (Chapel Hill: University of North Carolina Press, 1943); *The Colonial Search for a Southern Eden* (University: University of Alabama Press, 1953); and *The Dream of Prosperity in Colonial America* (New York: New York University Press, 1965). The best examination of Southern promotion literature is chap. 1 of Richard Beale Davis, *Intellectual Life in the Colonial South 1585–1763*, 3 vols. (Knoxville: University of Tennessee Press, 1978).

2. For *The Land of Cockaygne*, see J. A. W. Bennett and B. V. Smithers, eds., *Early Middle English Verse and Prose* (Oxford: Clarendon Press, 1966), 136–44; and a long selection (lacking 80 lines) in Celia and Kenneth Sisam, eds., *Oxford Book of Medieval English Verse* (Oxford: Clarendon Press, 1970), 159–63 and 578. George Boas, *Essays on Primitivism and Related Ideas in the Middle Ages* (Baltimore: Johns Hopkins Press, 1948), 167–68, has an excellent brief discussion. A. L. Morton, *The English Utopia* (London: Lawrence & Wishart, 1952) presents a full context for the poem. Two recent suggestive studies are Irene Howard, "The Folk Origins of 'The Land of Cokaygne,'" *Humanities Association Bulletin* 18 (1967): 72–79; and Geoffrey Bullough, "The Later History of Cockaigne," *Wiener Beitrage zur Englischen Philologie* 75 (1973): 22–35. For *Eastward Hoe!*, see *Ben Jonson*, ed. C. H. Herford and Percy Simpson, 11 vols. (Oxford: Clarendon Press, 1925–52), 4:569–70 (3.325–54), notes, 9:663–64, where Jonson's allusions to Hakluyt's *Principal Navigations* and More's *Utopia* are pointed out.

3. David Beers Quinn, ed., *The Roanoke Voyages 1584–1590*, 2 vols. (London: Hakluyt Society, 1955), 1:323. In all quotations, I have brought superscript letters down to the line, expanded abbreviations, and normalized *u* and *v*, *i*, and *j*.

4. Philip L. Barbour, ed., *The Jamestown Voyages Under the First Charter, 1606–1609*, 2 vols. (Cambridge: Hakluyt Society, 1969), 2:353, 372–73.

5. Henry Martin Dexter, ed., *Mourt's Relation or Journal of the Plantation at Plymouth* (Boston: J. K. Wiggin, 1865), 135–36.

6. Alexander Young, ed., *Chronicles of the Pilgrim Fathers* (Boston: Little and Brown, 1841), 292.

7. Barbour, *Jamestown Voyages*, 1:243.

8. Edward Arber and A. G. Bradley, eds., *Travels and Works of Captain John Smith*, 2 vols. (Edinburgh: John Grant, 1910), 1:207–8.

9. Young, *Pilgrim Fathers*, 372–73.

10. Christopher Levett, *A Voyage into New England* (London: William Jones, 1628). Reprinted in *Collections of the Massachusetts Historical Society*, 3d ser., 8 (1843): 159–90, at 179.

11. John Hammond, *Leah and Rachel, or the Two Fruitful Sisters Virginia and Maryland* (London, 1656), 6; and Benjamin Franklin, *Information to Those Who Would Remove to America* (1782), in Albert H. Smyth, ed., *The Writings of Benjamin Franklin*, 10 vols. (New York: Macmillan, 1905–7), 8:607. For a discussion of Hammond's promotion pamphlet, which contains the fullest seventeenth-century version of the American Dream, see J. A. Leo Lemay, *Men of Letters in Colonial Maryland* (Knoxville: University of Tennessee Press, 1972), 38–42, and 46–47.

12. Levett, *Voyage* (reprint), 182. George Alsop, in *A Character of the Province of Maryland* (1666), either echoes Levett or contradicts the same rumors. Lemay, *Men of Letters*, 55.

13. Everett Emerson, ed., *Letters from New England: The Massachusetts Bay Colony, 1629–1638* (Amherst: University of Massachusetts Press, 1976), 21.

14. Ibid., 36.

15. Ibid., 64.

16. Ibid., 68, 75, 78, and 75, respectively.

17. Arber and Bradley, *Travels and Works of Smith*, 2:954–55, 957.

18. William Wood, *New England's Prospect*, ed. Alden T. Vaughan (Amherst: University of Massachusetts Press, 1977), 20 and 67.

19. The earliest extant copy appears in *The Second Part of Merry Drollery* (London: [Printed by J. W. for P. H., 1661]), 91–93. I cite this text. See Case no. 132(2)(a). Arthur E. Case, *A Bibliography of English Poetical Miscellanies 1521–1750* (Oxford: Bibliographical Society, 1935). The song was reprinted in later editions of *Merry Drollery:* in 1670, on pp. 275–77 (Case no. 132[b]); in 1691, pp. 275–77 (Case no. 132[c]); and in Joseph Woodfall Ebsworth, ed., *Merry Drollery Compleat* (Boston; Lincolnshire: R. Roberts, 1875), 275–77. Charles H. Firth reprinted it from Ebsworth in *An American Garland: Being a Collection of Ballads Relating to America 1563–1759* (Oxford: Blackwell, 1915), 32–34.

Further, with a variant title ("The New England Ballad") and a variant first line ("Will you please to give ear . . .") the song appeared in at least five early-eighteenth-century song collections, including the largest and most popular, Thomas Durfey's *Wit and Mirth: or Pills to Purge Melancholy*, 6 vols. (London: W. Pearson for J. Tonson, 1719), 4:52–54. See no. 3976 in the "Index of First Lines" in Cyrus Lawrence Day and Elanore Boswell Murrie, *English Song Books 1561–1702* (London: Bibliographical Society, 1940), 389.

20. The tune given for *A Net for a Night-Raven* (London: For F. Coles, T. Vere, and J. Wright, [c. 1660]), Sabin 100502, is "Let us to Virginny go"; but this ballad is otherwise unknown. The tune given for *"The Sence of the House,"* in *Rump* (London, 1660), 1:101, is "The New England Psalm," which is also unknown. (Claude M. Simpson, *The British Broadside Ballad and Its Music* [New Brunswick: Rutgers University Press, 1966], 179, suggests that this tune is the same as "The Devil's Progress.") And the tune given for *The Quakers Farewel to England* (London, c. 1675), Wing Q23, reprinted in Joseph Woodfall Ebsworth, ed., *The Bagford Ballads* (Hertford: Ballad Society, 1878), 2:725–33, is "The Independents Voyage to New England," also otherwise unknown.

21. George Parker Winship, "Ballad Satirizing the Puritans," *Publications of the Colonial Society of Massachusetts* 26 (1924–26): 362–66.

22. The opening couplet is similar to "Glotonye's speech to "Ryot" in a sixteenth-century morality play: "In fayth to the new founde land let us go / For in england there is no remedy." George L. Frost and Ray Nash, "Good Order: A Morality Fragment," *Studies in Philology* 41 (1944): 490. Bertrand H. Bronson, *The Traditional Tunes of the Child Ballads*, 4 vols. (Princeton: Princeton University Press, 1959–72), 1:354–61; and Bronson, *The Singing Tradition of Child's Popular Ballads* (Princeton: Princeton University Press, 1976), 116.

23. "Verses on the Puritan Settlement of America, 1631," in P. A. Kennedy, ed., Thoroton Society, *Record Series* 21 (1962): 37–39.

24. This is the title of the copy in the Bodleian Library, Tanner MS, v. 306, fol. 286–87. See Margaret Crum, *The First-Line Index of English Poetry, 1500–1800, in Manuscripts of the Bodleian Library*, 2 vols. (Oxford: Clarendon, 1969), no. L 143. Samuel Eliot Morison, *Builders of the Bay Colony* (Boston: Houghton Mifflin, 1930), 384–386, accurately prints this manuscript.

25. *The Second Part of Merry Drollery* (1661), 103–5. And in Joseph Woodfall Ebsworth, ed., *Choyce Drollery . . . To Which are Added the Extra Songs of Merry Drollery, 1661* (Boston, Lincolnshire: R. Roberts, 1876), 243–47.

A fourth version, the Ashmoleian, was printed by G. D. Scull, "English Ballads about New England," *New England Historic and Genealogic Register* 36 (1882): 361–62, from Bodleian MS Ashmole 38, fol. 225 (Crum no. L 147). A fifth version, at the Public Record Office, was located and described by W. Noel Sainsbury, *Calendar of State Papers, Colonial Series, 1574–1660* (London: Longman, 1860), 180, who dated it "1634?" Entitled "A Propper Ballad, called the 'Sommons to New England,' to the Tune of 'The Townsman's Capp,'" it is printed in *Proceedings of the Massachusetts Historical Society* 5 (1860): 101–3. And, according to Ebsworth, *Choyce Drollery* (1876), 367, a sixth version, entitled "The Puritans of New England," is in the British Library, Harl. MS No. 6057, fol. 47. Firth, *American Garland*, 27–30, prints the Tanner MS copy, but emends it from the printed copy in *The Second Part of Merry Drollery*.

26. *An Invitation to Lubberland* is reprinted in Joseph Woodfall Ebsworth and William Chappell, eds., *The Roxburghe Ballads*, 8 vols. (Hertford: Ballad Society, 1871–95), 7:562–66. See also British Library, Department of Prints and Drawings, Division I, *Political and Personal Satires* (London: British Museum, 1890), 1:391, no. 704. Wing I 290. Stanza 6 anticipates the twentieth-century song, "Big Rock Candy Mountains": "The rivers run with claret fine, / The brooks with rich canary, / The ponds with other sorts of wine, / To make your hearts full merry: / Nay, more than this, you may behold, / The fountains flow with brand, / The rocks are like refined gold, / The hills are sugar-candy." For versions of "The Big Rock Candy Mountains," see George Milburn, *The Hobo's Hornbook* (New York: Ives Washington, 1930), 61–62, 87–89.

27. Charles H. Firth, "The Ballad History of the Reign of Charles I," *Transactions of the Royal Historical Society*, 3d ser., 6 (1912): 19–64, at 33, 35–38, briefly surveys the anti-puritan ballads. William P. Holden, *Anti-Puritan Satire 1572–1642* (New Haven: Yale University Press, 1954), provides a good overview. For specifics, see John Cleveland's "The Puritan," in Charles Mackay, ed., *Cavalier Songs and Ballads* (London: Bohn, 1863), 61–63; and "A Puritan of late," in *Merry Drollery*, 1661, reprinted in Ebsworth, *Choyce Drollery*, 195–96, and notes, 349–50. These satiric butts were also standard in the lubberland genre; cf. *An Invitation to Lubberland*.

28. Hyder E. Rollins, *An Analytical Index to the Ballad-Entries (1557–1709) in the Registers of the Company of Stationers of London* (1924; reprint, Hatboro, Pa.: Tradition Press, 1967), no. 929. A manuscript copy is in the Bodleian Library, Ashmole MSS, v. 26, fol. 37 (Crum no. M 597). It has been printed by Scull, "English Ballads about New England," 359; and by Morison, *Builders*, 45–46. The earliest extant printed version is in *Rump* (London, 1662), 1:1 (Case no. 128[c]). The song is also found in *Merry Drollery* (London, 1661), 91: *Merry Drollery Complete* (1670), 95; *Loyal Songs* (London, 1731), 1:4 (Case no. 128[d]). The *Merry Drollery* text has been accurately reprinted by Ebsworth in *Merry Drollery Compleat*, 95. Firth, *American Garland*, 25–26, prints the *Merry Drollery* text, but follows the accidentals of the *Rump* version. The song is listed in Harold Fletcher Books, "Rump Songs; an Index with Notes," *Publications of the Oxford Bibliographical Society* 5 (1940): pt. 4, p. 302, no. 140. Carleton Sprague Smith, "Broadsides and Their Music in Colonial America," in *Music in Colonial Massachusetts 1630–1820. I: Music in Public Places* (Boston: Colonial Society of Massachusetts

[v. 53 of its Publications], 1980), 165–66; and Firth, "Ballad History of the Reign of Charles I," 37–38, briefly discuss it.

29. The anonymous burlesque "The Little Old Sod Shanty on the Claim" is better known than the original "The Little Old Log Cabin in the Land" by W. S. Hays. See Louise Pound, "The Pedigree of a Western Song," *Modern Language Notes* 29 (1914): 30–31. Similarly, "Sweet Nebraska Land" or "Dakota Land" is better known than the original "Beulah Land." Richard E. Lingenfelter et al., eds., *Songs of the American West* (Berkeley and Los Angeles: University of California Press, 1968), 456–61.

30. The three copies of the *Rump* (1662), 1:1, at the Huntington Library contain identical texts. I quote from Huntington accession no. 79675.

31. Simpson, *British Broadside Ballad*, 713.

32. Rollins, *Analytical Index*, no. 2004. A manuscript version in the Bodleian, Ashmore MSS, 36, 37, fol. 100 (Crum no. Y 357) has been printed by Scull, "English Ballads about New England," 360–361, and by Morison, *Builders*, 62–63. Another manuscript, in a collection of songs made by Thomas Britton, c. 1682, was printed by E. F. Rimbault, *A Little Book of Songs and Ballads* (London: J. R. Smith, 1851), 183–86.

33. Printed versions appear in *Wit and Drollery* (London, 1661), 81–83 (Case 114[b]); in *The Second Part of Merry Drollery* (1661), 84–86; in *Merry Drollery Complete* (1670), 266–68. It also appears in the numerous editions of *Wit and Mirth*, e.g., 1719 edition, 3:119–21; Day and Murrie, *English Song-Books*, no. 4104, lists the various *Wit and Mirth* printings. Reprinted in Ebsworth, *Merry Drollery Compleat* (1875), 266–68.

34. Quoted from the Huntington Library copy (accession no. 55771) of *Merry Drollery Complete* (1670), 266.

35. Simpson, *British Broadside Ballad*, 275–76. Simpson notes that another broadside, *A Description of Old England*, has the same refrain, repeats some of the same stanzas, and was sung "To a pleasant new tune, Or, Is not Old England grown new."

36. Ebsworth, in *Merry Drollery Compleat* (1875), 394, and in *Choyce Drollery* (1876), 404; and Firth, *American Garland*, xxv–vi, both date it from 1643 or earlier.

37. See the *DNB* entries for Hamden and Pym.

38. *Rump* (1662), 1:95; Case 128(b). The three Huntington copies of *Rump* have identical texts, and I have used accession no. 79675. Firth, *American Garland*, 31, reprints the *Rump* text. The song also appeared in *Loyal Songs* (London, 1731), 1:92; see Brooks, "Rump Songs," p. 302, no. 142.

39. Huntington Library, accession no. HM16522, p. 73, where the reference is "To the same Tune." The previous song, "King Charles they say shall have his Crowne," p. 72, is "To the tune of Come buy my new Almanack, new." This manuscript version contains only four stanzas (the printed versions have five) and has many substantive variants.

40. See n. 19.

41. Firth, *American Garland*, xxvi. In his "Ballad History of the Reign of Charles I," 37, Firth suggests that it was published between 1620 and 1640.

42. Cf. "The Western Husband-man's Complaint in the late War" in Ebsworth, *Choyce Drollery* (1876), 57–59; and "A West-County Ballad," in Rimbault, *Little Book*, 122–24. Any use of "Countryman" in the title of a broadside suggested that the persona was a naif: see "The North-Countryman's Song," "The Countryman's Ramble through Bartholomew Fair," and "The Citizen's Vindication against the Downright Country-man (alias Boobee)," in Rimbault, *Little Book*, 151, 166; and in Ebsworth and Chappell, *Roxburghe Ballads*, 7:278, respectively.

43. The *Wit and Mirth* version updated the reference to "*Woodbury* Fair."

44. "England is the ringing island." *The Oxford Dictionary of English Proverbs*, ed. William George Smith, 3d ed., rev. F. P. Wilson (Oxford: Clarendon, 1970), 222. Cf. Thomas

Lechford, *Plain Dealing, or News from New England* (1642), ed. J. Hammond Trumbull (Boston: Wiggin & Lunt, 1867), 44.

45. William Bradford, *History of Plymouth Plantation 1620–1647*, ed. Worthington Chauncey Ford, 2 vols. (Boston: Houghton Mifflin, 1912), 1:402–3.

46. Young, *Pilgrim Fathers*, 255 n.; Bradford, *Plymouth Plantation*, 1:236 n.

47. Bradford, *Plymouth Plantation*, 2:212 n. See also Thomas Morton, *New English Canaan*, ed. Charles Francis Adams (Boston: Prince Society, 1883), 69–70, 322; and *Proceedings of the Massachusetts Historical Society* 5 (1860–62): 131.

48. Thaddeus M. Harris, *Memorials of the First Church in Dorchester* (Boston: Daily Advertiser, 1830).

49. Henry Wilder Foote, *Three Centuries of American Hymnody* (Cambridge: Harvard University Press, 1940), 30–32.

50. Percy A. Scholes, *The Puritans and Music in England and New England* (London: Oxford University Press, 1934), 258.

51. Ibid., 270–74.

52. Firth, *American Garland*, 25–26. See above, n. 27.

53. Firth, "Ballad History of the Reign of Charles I," 35–37.

54. In England, Edward Winslow confessed that "haveing been called to place of magistracie, he had sometimes married some." Bradford, *Plymouth Plantation*, 2:202. Lechford, *Plaine Dealing*, 86–87 and note.

55. See "A Puritan," in Ebsworth, *Choyce Drollery* (1876), 195–96, and Ebsworth's notes 349–50; and Firth, *American Garland*, 25 (second stanza of "The Zealous Puritan").

56. Frances Rose-Troup, *The Massachusetts Bay Company and Its Predecessors* (New York: Grafton Press, 1930).

57. Wood, *New England's Prospect*, 58.

58. Harris, *Memorials*; and *Memoirs of Roger Clap* (Boston: David Clapp, 1844), 39.

59. Hyder Edward Rollins, *Cavalier and Puritan: Ballads and Broadsides Illustrating the Period of the Great Rebellion 1640–1660* (New York: New York University Press, 1923), 31.

60. Although Carl Bridenbaugh has attributed this song to William Strode, Strode's only poem that resembles it is "A Devonshire Song," which tells of a countryman's visit to Plymouth, England. Bridenbaugh, *Vexed and Troubled Englishmen 1590–1642* (New York: Oxford University Press, 1968), 451–52; and *The Poetical Works of William Strode*, ed. Bertram Dobell (London: B. Dobell, 1907), 114–19, and 253.

61. Those who know the scholarship and the songs themselves may be surprised that I have not mentioned the fine lubberland burlesque, supposedly written in the 1650s, entitled "The Land of Cocaigne." Ebsworth and Chappell, *Roxburghe Ballads*, 7:568. Despite its use by Bullough, "Later History of Cockaigne," 30–31, I believe, for reasons of style, diction, and content, that it is a nineteenth-century creation.

62. "God's Country" was a common name for the West in nineteenth-century America. For one repeated use, see Martha L. Smith, *Going to God's Country*, intro. Clara E. Krefting (Boston: Christopher Publishing House, 1941), passim.

Chapter 2. The Colonist's Lot: Hardships and Hindrances

1. For "discommodities," see Levett, *Voyage*, 161, 182; John White, *The Planters Plea. On the Grounds of Plantations Examined and usuall objections Answered* (London: W. Iones, 1630). Reprinted in "Founding of Massachusetts," *Proceedings of the Massachusetts Historical Society* 62 (1930): 388–39; Francis Higginson, "Letters to His Friends in England" (1629), in *Letters*, ed. Emerson, 30, 36, 37; and Wood, *New England's Prospect*, 57. For "annoyances," see ibid., 59 and 65; and Lechford, *Plain Dealing*, 112.

2. Higginson, "Letters," 30 and 36; Smith, *Travels and Works*, 56, 61, 954; and Wood, *New England's Prospect*, pp. 38, 34.

3. Wood, *New England's Prospect*, 34. Thomas Hutchinson, *The History of the Colony and Province of Massachusetts-Bay*, ed. Lawrence Shaw Mayo, 3 vols. (Cambridge: Harvard University Press, 1936), 1:404.

4. Bradford, *Plymouth Plantation*, 1:364. Wood, *New England's Prospect*, 34. Most of Wood's chapter 4, *"Of the Nature of the Soil,"* 33–36, defends the quality of the grass.

5. Levett, *Voyage*, 181; White, *Planter's Plea*, 388; Higginson, "Letters," 36; Smith, *Travels and Works*, 952–53; Thomas Dudley, "Letter to the Countess of Lincoln, March, 1631," in *Letters from New England*, ed. Emerson, 68; Wood, *New England's Prospect*, 27; Morton, *New English Canaan*, 228; Lechford, *Plain Dealing*, 114; Henry Dunster and Thomas Weld, *New England's First Fruits* (1643), in *The Founding of Harvard College*, ed. Samuel Eliot Morison (Cambridge: Harvard University Press, 1935), 445; Edward Johnson, *Good News from New England* (London: M. Simmons, 1648), 9; and Bradford, *Plymouth Plantation*, 1:65.

6. Roger Williams, *A Key into the Language of America*, ed. John J. Teunissen and Evelyn J. Hinz (1643; reprint, Detroit, Mich.: Wayne State University Press, 1973), 157; Wood, *New England's Prospect*, 27–28, 29; Lechford, *Plain Dealing*, 114, sec. 11, n. 3.

7. For a general description, see Robert R. Walcott, "Husbandry in Colonial New England," *New England Quarterly* 9 (1936): 218–52, esp. 222–30.

8. John Winthrop, *Journal*, ed. James Savage, 2d ed. (Boston: Little, Brown, 1853), 1:246; Fulmer Mood, "John Winthrop, Jr., on Indian Corne," *New England Quarterly*, 10 (1937): 121–33, at 127. Esther S. Larson, ed., "Pehr Kalm's Description of Maize," *Agricultural History* 9 (1935): 98–117, at 107. Conway Zirkle, "To Plow or Not to Plow: Comment on the Planters' Problems," *Agricultural History* 43 (1969): 87–88. And William N. Parker, "A Note on Regional Culture in the Corn Harvest," *Agricultural History* 46 (1972): 181–89, at 182–83.

9. Winslow, *Good News from New England* (1624), in Young, *Pilgrim Fathers*, 370–71; Wood, *New England's Prospect*, 51 and 44. Mood, "John Winthrop, Jr.," 126 and 127. Morton, *New English Canaan*, 192, 198, aand 212; Winthrop, *Journal*, 2:113; and Johnson, *Good News*, 82, 85, and 114. *Dictionary of Americanisms on Historical Principles*, s.v. "corn," 6.(1) for *cornbird* and 6.(16) for *cornthief*. Peter N. Carroll, *Puritanism and the Wilderness*, 192. Larson, "Kalm's Description," 114. Nicholas P. Hardeman, *Shucks, Shocks, and Hominy Blocks: Corn as a Way of Life in Pioneer America* (Baton Rouge: Louisiana State University Press, 1981), 69, quotes the folk rhyme.

10. Francis Harper, ed., *The Travels of William Bartram* (New Haven: Yale University Press, 1958), 123–24. For a general account of the "enemies" of corn, see Hardeman, *Corn*, 185–209.

11. For the background, see Marion H. Gottfried, "The First Depression in Massachusetts," *New England Quarterly* 9 (1936): 655–78; and Darrett B. Rutman, "Governor Winthrop's Garden Crop: The Significance of Agriculture in the Early Commerce of Massachusetts Bay," *William and Mary Quarterly* 20 (1963): 396–415, esp. 397–402. *Winthrop Papers*, ed. Allyn Bailey Forbes et al., 5 vols. (Boston: Massachusetts Historical Society, 1929–47), 4:257; *Massachusetts Records*, 1:304; Winthrop, *Journal*, 2:13, 15; *Winthrop Papers*, 4:315, 314; and Lechford, *Plain Dealing*, 113.

12. Dunster and Weld, *First Fruits*, 444; Nathaniel Ward, *The Simple Cobler of Aggawam in America* (1647), ed. P. M. Zall (Lincoln: University of Nebraska Press, 1969), 49; and Winthrop to Sir Nathaniel Rich, *Winthrop Papers*, 3:166.

13. For Pond, see Emerson, *Letters*, 65; Winthrop, in ibid., 88; Wood, *New England's Prospect*, 71 (cf. 39); Nathaniel B. Shurtleff, ed., *Records of the Governor and Company of the Massachusetts Bay in New England* (Boston: William White, 1853), 1:294, 313 (hereafter called

Mass. Records); Winthrop, *Journal*, 1:331; Ward, *Simple Cobler*, 25–26; Lechford, *Plain Dealing*, 113; Dunster and Weld, *First Fruits*, 444. For White's loss of linen, see Lemay, *Men of Letters*, 16–17. Hooker, *A Survey of the Summe of Church-Discipline* (1648; reprint, New York: Arno Press, 1972), "Preface," sig. [4v]. The anti-Virginia ballad is *The Trappan'd Maiden* (London: W[illiam] O[lney], c. 1709?), Sabin 96474, in Firth, *American Garland*, 52. On the raising of hemp and flax, see Walcott, "Husbandry," 236–37.

   14. William Hubbard, *General History* (Boston: Massachusetts Historical Society, 1848), 238. Carl Bridenbaugh, *Fat Mutton and Liberty of Conscience: Society in Rhode Island, 1636–1690* (Providence: Brown University Press, 1974), 17, 14, 50–57. William Bradford, *The Collected Verses*, ed. Michael G. Runyon (St. Paul, Minn.: John Colet Press, 1974), 211, lines 131–37. Samuel Maverick, "Briefe Discription," *Proceedings of the Massachusetts Historical Society* 2d ser., 1 (1884–85): 231–49, at 235. Walcott, "Husbandry," 246, discusses the increase in sheep. Bridenbaugh, *Fat Mutton*, 56, quotes the "neere" 100,000.

   15. Higginson, "Letters," 32 (cf. 40); Wood, *New England's Prospect*, 36; *Winthrop Papers*, 3:167.

   16. Bradford, *Collected Verses*, 209, ll. 109–10. Johnson, *Good News* (1648), 10. For Brereton, Archer, and Rosier, see Charles H. Levermore, *Forerunners and Competitors of the Pilgrims and Puritans 1601–1625* (Brooklyn, N.Y.: N.E. Society of Brooklyn, 1912), 1:32–33; 42, 45, 52, 318–19, 321, 343, 347, 351. Smith, *Travels and Works*, 1:238–42, 254; and 2:944. Wood, *New England's Prospect*, 53–57. Dexter, *Mourt's Relation*, 60–61, 135–36. Williams, *Key*, 180–84. Morton, *New English Canaan*, 221–28. And Emerson, *Letters*, 61–64.

   17. Rutman, "Governor Winthrop's Garden Crop," maintains that "The crux of the economic problem facing the settlers [in the early 1640s] was the existence of an unsaleable agricultural surplus" (p. 400). When Johnson tells of the depression, he emphasizes the abundance of food, and Samuel Danforth makes the same observation (see pp. 42 and 69). Bradford, *Plymouth Plantation*, 1:324.

   18. Dean Albertson, "Puritan Liquor in the Planting of New England," *New England Quarterly* 23 (1950): 477–90. Smith, *Travels and Works*, 954–55; Bradford, *Plymouth Plantation*, 1:57, 164, 363–64; Dexter, *Mourt's Relation*, 18; and Wood, *New England's Prospects*, 37.

   19. *Winthrop Papers*, 5:323. *The Trappan'd Maiden* in Firth, *American Garland*, 52. Henry David Thoreau, *Walden*, ed. J. Lyndon Shanley (Princeton: Princeton University Press, 1971), 64. George Lyman Kittredge, "Dr. Robert Child the Remonstrant," *Publications of the Colonial Society of America* 21 (1919): 1–146, at 110. Mood, "John Winthrop, Jr.," 131–33. Raymond P. Stearns, *Science in the British Colonies of America* (Urbana: University of Illinois Press, 1970), 128–29, tells that Winthrop's beer from "maiz-bread" was tasted by members of the Royal Society on 11 March 1662/63, who judged it "a pale well-tasted middle Beer." Robert Beverley, *The History and Present State of Virginia*, ed. Louis B. Wright (Chapel Hill: University of North Carolina Press, 1947), 293. Larson, "Kalm's Description," 113. For apple cider, see Albertson, "Puritan Liquor," 480; Walcott, "Husbandry," 250; and the colonial Maryland folk ditty in Lemay, *Men of Letters*, [vii].

   20. Edmund S. Morgan, *Visible Saints: The History of a Puritan Idea* (1963; reprint, Ithaca: Cornell University Press, 1965), passim, but esp. 93–112. For the Puritans' own splendid presentation of their position (written in late 1636), see their answer to "Certain Proposals made by Lord Say, Lord Brooke, and other Persons of quality," and John Cotton's letter to Lord Say and Seal of 1636, appendixes 2 and 3 in Hutchinson, *Massachusetts-Bay*, 410–17. Fifty-one public confessions delivered in the church at Cambridge, Massachusetts, have just been edited with an excellent introduction; see George Selement and Bruce C. Woolley, eds., *Thomas Shepard's Confessions, Publications of the Colonial Society of Massachusetts* 58 (1981).

   21. Lechford, *Plain Dealing*, 7, 23, and 25. Editor Trumbull's splendid notes cite numerous analogues.

22. Winthrop, *Journal*, 2:238. Morgan, *Visible Saints*, 113–52, traces the decline of the church membership test through the late seventeenth century. Larzer Ziff, ed., *John Cotton on the Churches of New England* (Cambridge: Harvard University Press, 1968), 263–64.

23. Emerson, *Letters*, 65, 72, 78–79; Wood, *New England's Prospect*, 67; Smith, *Travels and Work*, 2:954–55.

24. Dexter, ed., *Mourt's Relation*, 150. Winthrop, *Journal*, 1:399–401; 2:39–40; and see the *Winthrop Papers*, 4:263–67, 314–16. Arthur Percival Newton sets forth the background of the remigration in *The Colonizing Activities of the English Puritans* (New Haven: Yale University Press, 1914), 249–56, 283–93, and 304–6.

25. Winthrop, *Journal*, 2:103–5, and 294; see also 2:25. Edward Johnson, *History of New England* (1654), ed. J. Franklin Jameson (New York: Scribners, 1910), 202. See also William L. Sachse, "The Migration of New Englanders to England, 1640–1660," *American Historical Review* 53 (1948): 251–78; idem, "Harvard Men in England, 1642–1714," *Publications of the Colonial Society of Massachusetts* 35 (for 1942–46 [1951]): 119–44; Harry S. Stout, "University Men in New England 1620–1660: A Demographic Analysis," *Journal of Interdisciplinary History* 4 (1974): 375–400; and idem, "The Morphology of Remigration: New England University Men and Their Return to England, 1640–1660," *Journal of American Studies* 10 (1976): 151–72.

26. Eliot, in Emerson, *Letters*, 106. An elaborately annotated edition of Eliot's letter is available in Franklin M. Wright, ed., "A College First Proposed, 1633: Unpublished Letters of Apostles Eliot and William Hammond to Sir Simonds D'Ewes," *Harvard Library Bulletin* 8 (1954): 255–82, at 270–76. Wood, *New England's Prospect*, 73–74.

27. *New Englands First Fruits* (London, 1643) has been reprinted four times: (1) *Massachusetts Historical Society Collections*, 1st ser., 1 (1792): 242–50; (2) New York: Sabin, 1865; (3) in Samuel Eliot Morison, *The Founding of Harvard College* (Cambridge: Harvard University Press, 1935), 420–47; and (4) in facsimile, Ann Arbor, Mich.: Readex, 1974. Although the Indian account in *First Fruits* was formerly attributed to John Eliot, Worthington C. Ford convincingly argued that Henry Dunster wrote both it and the account of the college. Ford also believed that Weld wrote the last part of the pamphlet and that Hugh Peter had a hand in the entire production. Ford, "The Authorship of *New Englands First Fruits*," *Proceedings of the Massachusetts Historical Society* 42 (1908–9): 259–66. Morison, *Founding*, 304–5, and Raymond P. Stearns, "The Weld-Peter Mission," *Publication of the Colonial Society of Massachusetts* 32 (1933–37): 218 n.1, both concur.

28. Quoted from Morison, *Founding*, 440–46, with the "objections" on 444–46 and the "remarkable passages" on 440–43.

29. On wolves, see Bradford, *Plymouth Plantation*, 1:366 and note; White, *Planter's Plea*, 388; Winslow, *Good Newes*, 370–71; Winthrop, *Journal*, 1:40, 44, 73, 137, etc.; Wood, *New England's Prospect*, 46 (for the quotation), 59, and 65; Morton, *New English Canaan*, 80. And in Emerson, *Letters*, see: Saltonstall, 92; Hammond, 111; Browne, 228; and Wiswall, 232.

30. White, *Planter's Plea*, 388; Higginson, "Letters," 36; Smith, *Travels and Works*, 2:955; Wood, *New England's Prospect*, 59, 65, 66; Morton, *New English Canaan*, 82–83; and Lechford, *Plain Dealing*, 112. For a survey of other rattlesnake stories in colonial America, see George Lyman Kittredge, "Letters of Samuel Lee to Samuel Sewall Relating to New England and the Indians," *Publications of the Colonial Society of Massachusetts* 14 (1911–13): 174–75, 183; James R. Masterson, "Colonial Rattlesnake Lore, 1714," *Zoologica* 23 (1938): 213–16; idem, "The Tale of the Living Fang," *American Literature* 11 (1939–40): 63–73; and "The Fascinating Rattlesnake," in Herbert Leventhal, *In the Shadow of the Enlightenment: Occultism and Renaissance Science in Eighteenth-Century America* (New York: New York University Press, 1976), 137–67.

31. Levett, *Voyage*, 181; White, *Planter's Plea*, 388; Higginson, "Letters," 36; Wood, *New*

England's Prospect, 59 (for the quotation), 67; Lechford, *Plain Dealing*, 112; Johnson, *Good News* (1648), 81; and Bradford, *Plymouth Plantation*, 1:366–67. For the reputation (and identification) of mosquitoes and America, see Lemay, *Men of Letters*, 83 and 234; and idem, "The Text, Tradition, and Themes of 'The Big Bear of Arkansas,'" *American Literature* 47 (1975–76): 326–27 and n. 11.

Chapter 3. The Earliest American Identities

1. Perry Miller, *Errand into the Wilderness* (Cambridge: Harvard University Press, 1956), 1–15, esp. 6 and 12. But Miller (seeming, in part, to contradict himself) also finds that the second generation, rather than the first, "Launched themselves upon the process of Americanization" (9). Robert Middlekauff, *The Mathers: Three Generations of Puritan Intellectuals 1596–1728* (New York: Oxford University Press, 1971), 96, 100. Conrad Cherry, "New England as Symbol: Ambiguity in the Puritan Vision," *Soundings: An Interdisciplinary Journal* 58 (1975): 348–62, at 353. And Sacvan Bercovitch, "Rhetoric and History in Early New England: The Puritan Errand Reassessed," in *Toward a New American Literary History: Essays in Honor of Arlin Turner*, ed. Louis J. Budd, Edwin H. Cady, and Carl L. Anderson (Durham: Duke University Press, 1980), 54–68, at 61.

2. Edward Johnson, *History*, 214, uses the phrase "a right N. E. man," cf. 60, 95, and 133. Some of the numerous possible references to Bradford and the other first-generation founders are given below. The very fact that Bradford wrote Book 1 of his history *Of Plymouth Plantation* in 1630 reveals he believed by that time that the colonization was successful and deserved the epic treatment he gave it. Bradford, *Plymouth Plantation*, 1:14.

3. *A Dictionary of Americanisms on Historical Principles*, ed. Mitford M. Mathews, 2 vols. (Chicago: University of Chicago Press, 1951), s.v. "corn," 8(2), gives 1784 as the earliest usage of "corn in the ear." (Hereafter Mathews is cited as *DA*.) When seventeenth- and eighteenth-century writers in England mentioned a racoon, they always thought it necessary to describe the American animal. *The Oxford English Dictionary*, ed. James A. H. Murray et al., 13 vols. (1884–1928; reprint, Oxford: At the University Press, 1933), s.v. "racoon." (Hereafter cited as *OED*.) *A Dictionary of American English on Historical Principles*, ed. William A. Craigie et al., 4 vols. (Chicago: University of Chicago Press, 1936–44), s.v. "racoon." (Hereafter cited as *DAE*.) And *DA*, s.v. "racoon."

4. Morgan, *Visible Saints*, 64–112; and see above, pp. 44–45.

5. Frank Strong, "A Forgotten Danger to the New England Colonies," American Historical Association *Report* for 1898 (Washington, D.C., 1899), 79–94, esp. 79–84. And Sachse, "Migration of New Englanders to England," 251–78. And see above, chap. 2, nn. 24 and 25.

6. 24 December 1630: "This day the wind came N.W., very strong, and some snow withal, but so cold as some had their fingers frozen, and in danger to be lost." 13 February 1637/8: "Three of them gate hame the next day over the ice, but their hands and feet frozen. Some lost their fingers and toes, and one died." Winthrop, *Journal*, 1:46, 302. Cf. above, chap. 2, n. 6.

7. Dr. Alexander Hamilton, *Itinerarium*, ed. Carl Bridenbaugh (Chapel Hill: University of North Carolina Press, 1948), 15. T. B. Thorpe, "The Big Bear of Arkansas," in *The Norton Anthology of American Literature*, ed. Hershel Parker et al., 2 vols. (New York: W. W. Norton, 1979), 1:1470.

8. Winthrop, *Journal*, 1:128, 152–53, 318, 330. Edward Johnson, "Woburn Town Records," in *Woburn Journal* (1888), 17 April 1651; 14 February 1652. Walcott, "Husbandry," 240.

9. Al Capp's comic strip, "Lil' Abner," featured these moonshiners; of course Billy De Beck's "Snuffy Smith" often carries his jug.

10. The Geneva Bible gloss on Amos 5:19. *The Geneva Bible: A Facsimile of the 1560 edition* (Madison: University of Wisconsin Press, 1969), 371.

11. Lemay, *Men of Letters*, 77–93.

12. A mideighteenth-century quatrain satirized Col. Eliphalet Dyer and the Susquehanna Company: "Canaan of old, as we are told, / When it did rain down manna, / Wa'nt half as good, for heavenly food. / As Dyer makes Susquehanna." Benson J. Lossing, *Pictorial Field-Book of the Revolution*, 2 vols. (New York: Harper, 1855), 1:347n. Another popular burlesque, James Murray's supposed letter to the Reverend Mr. Boyd, was reprinted in the *Pennsylvania Gazette*, 3 November 1737, and in the *New York Gazette*, 7 November 1737. William Byrd satirized primitivism and the "lubberland" of North Carolina. *The Prose Works of William Byrd of Westover*, ed. Louis B. Wright (Cambridge: Harvard University Press, 1966), 180 and 248. Robert Micklus, "'The History of the Tuesday Club': A Mock-Jeremiad of the Colonial South," *William and Mary Quarterly* 40 (1983): 42–61. Franklin, "Information," in *Works*, 8:603–14. In the cartoon strip "Peanuts" (June 1981), Snoopy set up as a real estate developer in the barren desert near Needles, California.

13. For a recent study of "Starving to Death on a Government Claim," see Jan Harold Brunvand, "'The Lane County Bachelor': Folksong or Not," in *Readings in American Folklore*, ed. Jan H. Brunvand (New York: W. W. Norton, 1979), 289–308. Brunvand, p. 290, cites two authorities who claim that the song is "a typical example of the Western folk worldview." Duncan Emrich, ed., *American Folk Poetry: An Anthology* (Boston: Little, Brown, 1974), 627–32. Richard E. Ligenfelter, Richard Dwyer, and David Cohen, eds., *Songs of the American West* (Berkeley and Los Angeles: University of California Press, 1968), 456–61. And Roger Welsch, *Sweet Nebraska Land* (Folkways FH5337, 1965). Ditmar Meidell, "Oleana," in *Norwegian Emigrant Songs and Ballads*, ed. Theodore Blegan and Martin B. Ruud (Minneapolis: University of Minnesota Press, 1936), 187–98. "Amerikavisan," in *Swedish Emigrant Ballads*, ed. Robert L. Wright (Lincoln: University of Nebraska Press, 1965), 37–39. "Skada," *Songs of the North Star State*, comp. Gene Bluestein (Folkways FA 2132, 1962).

14. Samuel S. Cox, *Why We Laugh* (1880; reprint, New York: Benjamin Blom, 1969), 215–20. J. A. Leo Lemay, "The Text, Tradition and Themes of 'The Big Bear of Arkansas,'" *American Literature* 47 (1975–76): 324–29. F. R. Rogers, "The Road to Reality: Burlesque Travel Literature and Mark Twain's *Roughing It*," *Bulletin of the New York Public Library* 67 (1963): 155–68.

15. Louise Pound, "The Pedigree of a 'Western Song,'" *Modern Language Notes* 29 (1914): 30–31. Lemay, *Men of Letters*, 90–91.

16. Rutland, "Governor Winthrop's Garden Crop," 402, 406, 407, 411n, and 414. *Winthrop Papers*, 2:320. Stephen Vincent Benét, *Western Star* (New York: Farrar & Rinehart, 1943), 116. For corn's identification with New England, see "Supplies of the Larder," in Alice Morse Earle, *Customs and Fashions in Old New England* (New York: Charles Scribner's Sons, 1893), 148–50.

17. J. A. Leo Lemay, "The American Origins of 'Yankee Doodle,'" *William and Mary Quarterly*, 3d ser., 33 (1976): 435–64, at 447–51. *The Papers of Benjamin Franklin*, ed. Leonard W. Labaree, William B. Willcox et al. (New Haven: Yale University Press, 1959–), 13:7. Allen Walker Read, "Boucher's Linguistic Pastoral of Colonial Maryland," *Dialect Notes* 6 (1933): 353–63. Lemay, "The Contexts and Themes of 'The Hasty Pudding,'" *Early American Literature*, 17 (1982): 3–23. *The Adventures of Jonathan Corncob* (1787), ed. Noel Perrin (Boston: David Godine, 1976).

18. Peter White, *Benjamin Tompson: Colonial Bard* (University Park: Pennsylvania State University Press, 1980), 84, ll. 1–3. Johnson, *History*, 85, 115, 154, and 210. In 1708, Sarah

Kemble Knight told an anecdote about Connecticut justices who built a pumpkin bench. See *The Journal of Madame Knight*, ed. George Parker Winship (1920; reprint; New York: Peter Smith, 1935), 35. Henry Hulton's parody of "The Liberty Song" (*Boston Gazette*, 26 September 1768) opens "Come shake your dull noddles, ye Pumpkins, and bawl." And Samuel Peters, in his mock *History of Connecticut* (1781) calls the New Englanders "pumpkin heads." See the *DAE* and *DA* for other references. It also seems significant that the nursery rhyme "Peter, Peter, pumpkin eater" first appeared in Boston. See Iona and Peter Opie, *The Oxford Dictionary of Nursery Rhymes* (London: Oxford University Press, 1975), 347. For the role of pumpkins in New England foods, see Earle, *Customs and Fashions*, 150–53. And for a splendid tribute to pumpkin pie, see "Josh Billings" [Henry Wheeler Shaw], *Old Probability: Perhaps Rain—Perhaps Not* (New York: G. W. Carleton, 1875), 12. *The Papers of Benjamin Franklin*, 3:453.

19. Tompson, "The Prologue," l.13, to *New Englands Crisis*, in *Benjamin Tompson: Colonial Bard*, ed. White, 84. [John Wise], *A Word of Comfort to a Melancholy Country* (Boston, 1721), 9. Even Johnson, writing in 1651, could think of 1638 as "the glorious days of New England." *History*, 183; and Bradford, in 1654, thought of the earlier "happy and blessed time." Bradford, *The Collected Verse*, 220.

20. Winthrop, *Journal*, 2:346–49. *Memoirs of Roger Clap* (Boston: David Clapp, 1844), 19–20, 30–31, and 42. Johnson, *History*, 25 and 212.

21. Smith, *Travels and Works*, 88; cf. 83, 93, etc.

22. *Winthrop Papers*, 2:136. Smith, *Travels and Works*, 948 and 782.

23. Bradford, *Plymouth Plantation*, 1:104–5, 109, 407; 2:4–6. Thomas Hooker, *A Survey*, sig. [a4ᵛ].

24. George Sandys, trans., *Metamorphoses* (London: W. Stansby, 1626), dedication. See Richard Beale Davis, "American in George Sandys' 'Ovid,'" *William and Mary Quarterly* 4 (1947): 297–304. William S. Powell, *John Pory, 1572–1636; The Life and Letters of a Man of Many Parts* (Chapel Hill: University of North Carolina Press, 1977), 109. Smith, *Travels and Works*, 622.

25. Winthrop, *Journal*, 2:363. J. A. Leo Lemay, "The Tall tales of a Colonial Frontiersman," *Western Pennsylvania Historical Magazine* 64 (1981): 44–45.

26. The Englishman was Paul Whitehead. Franklin, *Papers*, 20:439. For the context, see J. A. Leo Lemay, "Benjamin Franklin," in *Major Writers of Early American Literature*, ed. Everett Emerson (Madison: University of Wisconsin Press, 1972), 227–32, at 230.

27. See above, chap. 1, for the anti-American satires. The lead essays (which I believe are by Franklin) in the *Pennsylvania Gazette*, 20 April and 4 May 1732, reflect American resentment of British condescension. The best statement of resentment is Franklin's "Defense of the Americans," 9 May 1759. Franklin, *Papers*, 8:340–56. See also Lemay, *Men of Letters*, 86–87.

28. In "The Appalachian Backgrounds of Billy De Beck's Snuffy Smith," *Appalachian Journal* 4 (1977): 120–32, M. Thomas Inge shows De Beck's familiarity with the local-color realists, including Mary Noailles Murfree, and with the humorists of the Old South, including George Washington Harris. For twentieth-century literature portraying the type, see Sylvia Jenkins Cook, *From Tobacco Road to Route 66: The Southern Poor White in Fiction* (Chapel Hill: University of North Carolina Press, 1976).

29. The standard survey is Shields McIlwaine, *The Southern Poor-White from Lubberland to Tobacco Road* (Norman: University of Oklahoma Press, 1939). For the yokel persona in nineteenth-century American literature, see Mody C. Boatright, *Folk Laughter on the American Frontier* (New York: Collier Books, 1961), esp. chap. 1, "Some Mythology of the Frontier," and my "The Text, Tradition, and Themes of 'The Big Bear of Arkansas.'" David Bertelson, *The Lazy South* (New York: Oxford University Press, 1967), surveys the early

literature, but he did not know of the writings of Bolling and Cradock; see my "Southern Colonial Grotesque: Robert Bolling's 'Neanthe,' " *Mississippi Quarterly* 35 (1982): 97–126. For yokels in colonial New England and the Middle Colonies, see Lemay, "The American Origins of 'Yankee Doodle,' " 435–64; idem., "The Tall Tales," 33–46; Knight 25, cf. 43.

30. Franklin, *Writings*, 8:607.

31. Bradford, *Plymouth Plantation*, 1:124.

32. Ibid., 2:352. Bradford wrote Book 1 of his *History of Plymouth Plantation* in 1630 and Book 2 between 1646 and 1650. See 1:14, 16; 2:219 and 394.

33. Phillip Stubbes, *Anatomy of the Abuses in England* (1583), ed. Frederick J. Furnivall (1877–79; reprint, Vaduz, Liecht.: Kraus, 1965), 146–50, condemned the Lord of Mis-rule and the May Day celebrations. In reply to the Puritans' writing and preaching, James I, on 24 May 1618, in *The Kings Majesties Declaration to His Subjects Concerning Lawful Sports* (London: B. Norton, 1618), 7, encouraged games on Sundays and specified: "After the end of Divine Service, Our good people be not disturbed, letted, or discouraged . . . from having of May-Games, Whitson Ales, and Morris dances, and the setting up of May-poles and other sports therewith used." The Royalist poet Richard Corbett, in "An Exhortation to Mr. John Hammond" (1648), satirized the puritan Hammond's cutting down a maypole. *The Poems of Richard Corbett*, ed. J. A. W. Bennett and H. R. Trevor-Roper (Oxford: Clarendon Press, 1955), 51–56, and notes, 130–31.

34. Bradford, *Plymouth Plantation*, 2:48–51. Hawthorne, "The May-Pole of Merry Mount," in *Twice-Told Tales*, ed. J. D. Crowley, Centenary ed. (Columbus: Ohio State University Press, 1974), 9:54–67. See Richard Clark Sterne, "Puritans at Merry Mount: Variations on a Theme," *American Quarterly* 22 (1970): 846–58; John P. McWilliams, "Fictions of Merry Mount," *American Quarterly* 29 (1977): 3–30; Michael Zuckerman, "Pilgrims in the Wilderness: Community, Modernity, and the Maypole at Merry Mount," *New England Quarterly* 50 (1977): 255–77; and especially Robert D. Arner's insightful articles, "Mythology and the Maypole of Merrymount: Some Notes on Thomas Morton's 'Rise Oedipus,' " *Early American Literature* 6 (1971): 156–64; and "Pastoral Celebration and Satire in Thomas Morton's *New English Canaan*," *Criticism* 16 (1974): 127–31.

35. The modern Thanksgiving Day became a cultural institution during the first half of the nineteenth century. In his splendid study *The Fast and Thanksgiving Days of New England* (Boston: Houghton, Mifflin, 1895), William De Loss Love did his best to establish a seventeenth-century date for an annual thanksgiving day (see esp. pp. 241–49), but he only proves that it was a movable feast.

36. Smith, *Oxford Dictionary of English Proverbs*, 612.

37. William Meade, *Old Churches, Ministers, and Families of Virginia*, 2 vols. (Philadelphia: Lippincott, 1861), 1:475.

Chapter 4. Who Wrote the Song?

1. Justin Winsor, "The Literature of the Colonial Period," in *The Memorial History of Boston . . . 1630–1880*, ed. Winsor, 4 vols. (Boston: Ticknor, 1880), 1:460. Instead of quoting from "New England's Annoyances," Winsor uses lines 3–6 of Tompson's "Prologue." White, *Benjamin Tompson*, 84.

2. White, *Benjamin Tompson*, 160 nn. 2 and 5. Neither Howard Judson Hall, ed., *Benjamin Tompson . . . His Poems* (Boston: Houghton Mifflin Co., 1924), nor Peter White mentions Winsor's attribution of "New England's Annoyances" to Tompson.

3. Wood, *New England's Prospect*, 3–6.

4. Ibid. See also Charles Deane, ed., *Wood's New Englands Prospect* (Boston: Prince Society, 1865), ix–x.

5. Wood, *New England's Prospect*, 4–5.

6. See the *DAB* account of Morton by James T. Adams; Donald F. Connors, *Thomas Morton* (New York: Twayne, 1969); Arner, "Mythology and the Maypole of Merrymount," 156–64; Arner's "Pastoral Celebration and Satire in Thomas Morton's *New English Canaan*," 217–31; and McWilliams, "Fictions of Merry Mount," 3–30, esp. 4–15.

7. The *DAB* account is by Raymond Phineas Stearns. See also Ford, "Authorship," 259–66; and Stearns, "The Weld-Peter Mission to England," 188–246. Unfortunately, Zoltan Haraszti in *The Enigma of the Bay Psalm Book* (Chicago: University of Chicago Press, 1956) was not able to shed any light upon which psalms Weld wrote.

8. Raymond Phineas Stearns wrote the *DAB* account of Peter, the standard biography, *The Strenuous Puritan: Hugh Peter, 1598–1660* (Urbana: University of Illinois Press, 1954), and the most pertinent single article, "Hugh Peter was a Wit," *Proceedings of the American Antiquarian Society* 77 (1967): 13–34.

9. Edward H. Dewey wrote the *DAB* account and Samuel Eliot Morison treated Ward in *Builders of the Bay Colony*, 217–43. The most interesting accounts of Ward's style are Zdenck Vancura, "Baroque Prose in America," *Studies in English*, Charles University (Prague), 4 (1933): 39–58; Robert D. Arner, "The Simple Cobler of Aggawam: Nathaniel Ward and The Rhetoric of Satire," *Early American Literature* 5, iii (1970–71): 3–16; William J. Scheick, "Nathaniel Ward's Cobler as 'Shoem-Aker,'" *English Language Notes* 9 (1971): 100–102; Scheick, "The Widower Narrator in Nathaniel Ward's *The Simple Cobler of Aggawam in America*," *New England Quarterly* 47 (1974): 87–96; Jean F. Beranger, "Voices of Humor in Nathaniel Ward," *Studies in American Humor* 2 (October 1975): 96–104; and James Egan, "Nathaniel Ward and the Marprelate Tradition," *Early American Literature* 15 (1980): 59–71.

10. Kenneth Ballard Murdock wrote the *DAB* account. Murdock's *Handkerchiefs from Paul* (1927; reprint, New York: Garrett Press, 1970), 101–11, reprints Danforth's almanac verse (quotations from 105, 106).

11. Biographical facts about Johnson were first assembled by William Frederick Poole in the introduction to his excellent edition of Johnson's *History*, published as *The Wonder-Working Providences of Sions Saviour in New England* (Andover, Mass.: Warren F. Draper, 1867). Samuel Sewall added a few facts in *The History of Woburn, Middlesex County, Massachusetts* (Boston: Wiggin and Lunt, 1868), 73–76. The great resource for Johnson's later life, his "Woburn Town Records, 1640–1672," was printed in the *Woburn Journal* in 1888, with notes by Edward F. Johnson and William R. Cutter (see the notebook of clippings from the *Woburn Journal* at Harvard University, shelf number US13530.3F*). Samuel Eliot Morison wrote the *DAB* sketch of Johnson. For a bibliography, see "Writings about Edward Johnson, 1814–1975" in *Early Puritan Writers: A Reference Guide*, ed. Edward J. Gallagher and Thomas Werge (Boston: G. K. Hall, 1976), 127–48, which omits the "Woburn Town Records."

12. James Savage, *Collections of the Massachusetts Historical Society* 28 [3d ser., v. 8] (1843): 288, said it was "much in the style of Johnson's Wonder-working Providences." Harold S. Jantz, *The First Century of New England Verse* (1943; reprint, New York: Russell and Russell, 1962), 243–45, and 436–37, again suggested it was by Johnson; and Edward J. Gallagher, ed., *Wonder-Working Providences . . .* and *Good News From New England* (1648; reprint, Delmar, N.Y.: Scholars' Facsimiles & Reprints, 1974), x–xv, convincingly argues the case.

13. Jantz, *First Century*, 436–39.

14. For the "Woburn Town Records," see n. 9. Jantz, *First Century*, 242–43, 436.

15. Jantz, *First Century*, 245, 503.

16. Harold S. Jantz, "American Baroque: Three Representative Poets," in *Discoveries & Considerations: Essays on Early American Literature & Aesthetics Presented to Harold Jantz*, ed. Calvin Israel (Albany: State University of New York Press, 1976), 3–23, at 15. One nineteenth-century scholar who denied that Johnson had a sense of humor considered and rejected the attribution of "New England's Annoyances" to Johnson:

"Our Forefathers' Song" of which the author is unknown but which was composed about the year of Johnson's arrival in America [1630] has a sprightliness of composition which inclines the reader to the impression that it could not have been written by him. Johnson is always serious—and lines like those of which the prelude is, "New England's annoyances you that would know them, / Pray ponder these verses which briefly doth show them;" and whose jingle is illustrated by the following: "If fresh meat be wanting, to fill up our dish, / We have carrots and turnips as much as we wish; / And is there a mind for a delicate dish / We repair to the clam banks, and *there* we catch fish;" while they could not have been the production of the author of "Wonder-Working Providence," nor suggested to him a model to follow, yet are part of colonial poetry, and show the disposition of another class of mind to marry its ideas to verse, if not "immortal" at least entertaining (John D. Washburn, "Remarks on Early Poets and Poetry of New England, with a sketch of the life and poetry of Edward Johnson," *Proceedings of the American Antiquarian Society*, No. 69 (April 1877): 14–32, at 17–18.)

17. All quotations from the *History* are from Jameson's edition; those from *Good News From New England* (London: M. Simmons, 1648) are from the original (Huntington copy, accession no. 9154).

18. William Otis Bradley, *American Verse, 1625–1807* (New York: Moffatt and Yard, 1909), 5–8, commented on the striking portrayal of New England's winter, which he thought anticipated the appreciation found in Whittier's fine poem "Snowbound" (1866). Larzer Ziff, *Puritanism in America: New Culture in a New World* (New York: Viking, 1973), 125–27, also argues that, for Johnson and the Fireside School of nineteenth-century poets, "New England nature validates New England ideals" and points out that the climate became for New Englanders "a metaphor of their sound condition."

19. Rutman, "Governor Winthrop's Garden Crop," confirms Johnson's portrait of the general abundance of foods in the early 1640s. See above, n. 16 in chap. 3.

20. J. Franklin Jameson, *The History of Historical Writing in America* (Boston: Houghton, Mifflin, 1891), 29–40. Michael Kraus, *The Writing of American History* (Norman: University of Oklahoma Press, 1953), 27–28. Richard S. Dunn, "Seventeenth-Century English Historians of America," in *Seventeenth-Century America: Essays in Colonial History*, ed. James Morton Smith (Chapel Hill: University of North Carolina Press, 1959), 195–225, at 204–6. And Harvey Wish, *The American Historian: A Social Intellectual History of the Writing of the American Past* (New York: Oxford University Press, 1960), 15–16. Johnson's use of a mythic structure rather than a factually accurate account even makes some historians ignore him. Charles Francis Adams, *Massachusetts: Its Historians and Its History* (Boston: Houghton, Mifflin, 1893), omits Johnson. Peter Gay, *A Loss of Mastery: Puritan Historians in Colonial America* (Berkeley and Los Angeles: University of California Press, 1966), 53, makes only a passing reference to him.

21. James, *History of Historical Writing*, 9–10, prints the poem. I have added punctuation for clarity.

22. Cf. Jantz, "American Baroque," 14. Gallagher explains that Johnson "is not interested in the physical realities of the New England experience in themselves, but in the symbolic and spiritual meanings of that experience." Edward J. Gallagher, "An Overview of Edward Johnson's *Wonder-Working Providence*," *Early American Literature* 5 (1971): 37. In "The *Wonder-Working Providence* as Spiritual Biography," *Early American Literature* 10 (1975): 75–87, Gallagher points out that Johnson evidently fabricates an incident to make the book's structure conform more closely to the puritan paradigm of the steps to salvation (p. 83), and he shows how Johnson "forsakes strict chronology as a principle or organization for a pattern that would make the New England experience more recognizable to his readers" (p. 84).

23. Johnson's unique usage of "Clambanks" as a fish (shellfish? clams?) may explain why stanza 9 has evidently degenerated in the oral tradition.

24. In 1867, William E. Poole pointed out that Johnson's own title was evidently "The Wonder Working Providences of Sion's Saviour in New England." See William L. Williamson, "An Early Use of Running Title and Signature Evidence in Analytical Bibliography," *Library Quarterly* 40 (1970): 245–49.

25. Bradford, however, uses "scum" in a similar context: "Morton would entertain any, how vile soever, and all the scume of the countrie, or any discontente, would flock to him from all places." Bradford, *Plymouth Plantation*, 2:54.

26. Here Johnson specifically condemns the puritan frontiersmen "whose over eager pursuit of the fruits of the earth made some of them many times run out so far in this Wilderness, even out of the sweet sound of the silver Trumpets blown by the laborious Ministers of Christ, forsaking the assembly of the Lords people, to celebrate their Sabbaths in the chimney-corner, horse, kine, sheep, goats, and swine being their most indeared companions, to travel with them to the end of their pilgrimage" (253; cf. 234). Johnson's condemning the frontiersman might seem to contradict his celebration of New England's westward expansion. Lucy Lockwood Hazard first pointed out his praise of the frontier movement and first connected him with such later figures in American literature as Whitman. Harold Jantz and Roderick Nash have made similar observations. But Alan Heimert has explained the seeming contradiction. Johnson's wilderness was both the actual American wilderness (thus the Puritans' idea of the wilderness "came out of" the American experience) and the theological "desert Wilderness." It was necessary that they conquer the wilderness physically and, simultaneously, spiritually. The latter could only be accomplished by groups who would create churches at the same time that they created gardens in the wilderness. And Edward J. Gallagher shows how Johnson uses the "desert Wilderness" surroundings of New Englanders as a metaphor for mortification, an essential step in their progress toward salvation. Hazard, *The Frontier in American Literature* (New York: Crowell, 1927), 174–75. Jantz, *First Century*, 240. Nash, *Wilderness and the American Mind* (New Haven: Yale University Press, 1967), 37. Heimert, "Puritanism, the Wilderness, and the Frontier," *New England Quarterly* 26 (1953): 361–82, at 361, 367–69, and 376. And Gallagher, "The *Wonder-Working* Providence as Spiritual Biography," 75–87, at 82. For attitudes toward the frontiersman, see also Lemay, "The Frontiersman from Lout to Hero: Notes on the Significance of the Comparative Method and the Stage Theory in Early American History and Culture," *Proceedings of the American Antiquarian Society* 88 (1979): 187–224.

27. Jantz, *First Century*, 240, comments that Johnson "must have known Vergil well—and in the original, perhaps also Homer; for he not only had a thorough understanding of epic principles, he was also perhaps the first writer in English to make a successful transfer of the Homeric dactylic rhythm to our language." See also Cecilia Tichi, *New World, New Earth: Environmental Reform in American Literature from the Puritans through Whitman* (New Haven: Yale University Press, 1979), 39.

28. Gallagher, "The *Wonder-Working Providence* as Spiritual Biography," 76, 79–80, shows the puritan background of the "Souldiers of Christ" metaphor, documents Johnson's pervasive use of the tradition, and explains how it is "an emblem for the spiritual life."

29. Johnson also celebrates the progress of American civilization, including the development of numerous specialized trades in New England. So he devotes a long detailed catalogue to the gamut of New England occupations (248). But this passage follows his description of agricultural products as New England's "staple-commodity" (246–47). Cf. Tichi, *New World, New Earth*, 60–62.

30. In the best examination of Johnson's theology, Sacvan Bercovitch demonstrates Johnson's key role in grappling with the question of American identity. Bercovitch concludes that "this first history of Massachusetts vividly formulates the Puritan concept of the colonial venture, and establishes a pattern which may be traced in secular form through many of the subsequent urgent and obsessive definitions of the meaning of America." Bercovitch, "The

Historiography of Johnson's *Wonder-Working Providence*," *Essex Institute Historical Collections* 104 (1968): 138–61, at 161. Gallagher, in "An Overview," 47–48; and in "The Case of the *Wonder-Working Providence*," *Bulletin of the New York Public Library* 77 (1973): 10–27 at 19, 26–27, also argues that Johnson wrote "the first sustained mythicizing of the American experience" (19).

31. For the criticisms, see above n. 20. In 1878, Moses Coit Tyler appreciated Johnson's humor and some aspects of his prose, but condescendingly condemned him for his quaintness, Puritanism, and poetry. The first person to express enthusiasm for Johnson's splendid control was Harold Jantz. Norman Grabo (1962) added a brief appreciation of his artistic rhetorical strategy. And Ursula Brumm, in 1969, wrote a detailed analysis of three passages in Johnson. Recently, Edward J. Gallagher (1971, 1973, and 1975) has written three appreciations of Johnson's rhetorical achievement. Tyler, *A History of American Literature, 1607–1765* (1878; reprint, Ithaca: Cornell University Press, 1949). Jantz, "First Century," 239–45. Grabo, "The Veiled Vision: The Role of Aesthetics in Early American Intellectual History," *William and Mary Quarterly* 19 (1962): 439–510. Brumm, "Edward Johnson's Wonder-Working Providence and the Puritan Conception of History," *Jahrbuch für Amerikastudien* 14 (1969): 140–51. And Gallagher, "An Overview," "The Case," and "The *Wonder-Working Providence* as Spiritual Biography."

32. Poole, "Introduction," xxxix. Tichi, *New World, New Earth*, 44, 47.

33. See my remarks on the meaning of *American* and on the American identity in "The Frontiersman From Lout to Hero," 219–21; and see above, pp. 60–62.

34. John Eccles Trimpey, in the only article devoted specifically to this poem, praises especially the first four stanzas, which he believed were written by Johnson. Trimpey, "Literary Merit in Edward Johnson's Poem 'The Wonder Working Providences of Christ,'" *Publications of the Arkansas Philological Association* 4 (1978): 58–65. On the penitential tradition see Helen C. White, "Some Continuing Traditions in English Devotional Literature," *PMLA* 57 (1942): 966–80, at 974–75. See also the comments on Wyatt's penitential psalms in R. A. Rebholz, *Sir Thomas Wyatt: The Complete Poems* (New Haven: Yale University Press, 1978), 452–55.

35. The editions are listed in Jean Robertson, ed., *Nicholas Breton: Poems Not Hitherto Reprinted* (Liverpool: Liverpool University Press, 1967), xcii; and Robertson argues for Breton's authorship, xciii–xcviii. Mary Shakeshaft, "Nicholas Breton's *The Passion of a Discontented Mind*: Some New Problems," *Studies in English Literature, 1500–1900* 5 (1965): 165–74, pointed out that Ellis adapted the poem; and Edward Doughtie, "Nicholas Breton and Two Songs by Dowland," *Renaissance News* 17 (1964): 1–3, first noticed that John Dowland borrowed stanzas 1, 2, and 11 from *The Passion* for song no. 10 in *A Pilgrimes Solice* (London: W. Barclay, 1612). Dowland's borrowed stanzas are reprinted in E. H. Fellowes, ed., *English Madrigal Verse, 1588–1632*, 3d ed., revised by Frederick W. Sternfeld and David Greer (Oxford: Clarendon Press, 1967), 495; and by Edward Doughtie, *Lyrics from English Airs, 1596–1622* (Cambridge: Harvard University Press, 1970), 407–8. Doughtie argues that the poem is by Essex and prints variants among the manuscript and printed texts, pp. 613–15.

36. I have compared the Harvard copy of the 1621 edition (available on microfilm from University Microfilms) with Johnson's text and noted the following seventeen substantive differences (1621 edition before the closing half-bracket; Johnson after): (line) 2. with] in; 2. sinnes] sin; 5. despaire] lament; 6. sorrow, griefe, and care] sorrows sad relent; 9. my] with; 9. with] is not; 9. is not prevented] prevented; 10. For] Yet; 11. Thus] So; 11. cares] care; 15. do] doth; 16. Feares] Fear; 16. should] shall; 18. Teares] Christ; 21. workes] work; 24. As] That; 24. will] can.

37. In a letter of 7 February 1968, Professor Harold S. Jantz suggested to me that Johnson must have borrowed the first three stanzas of the poem.

38. Squire, in the *DNB* sketch of Dowland.

39. The importance of the pilgrim motif in Puritanism is set forth by William Haller, *The Rise of Puritanism* (New York: Columbia University Press), 147ff. The *locus classicus* of the motif in English literature is, of course, John Bunyan's *Pilgrim's Progress*. Samuel C. Chew surveys the art and literature of the motif in *The Pilgrimage of Life* (New Haven: Yale University Press, 1962). J. Paul Hunter, in *The Reluctant Pilgrim: Defoe's Emblematic Method and Quest for Form in Robinson Crusoe* (Baltimore: Johns Hopkins Press, 1966), entitles chapter 5 "Metaphor, Type, Emblem, and the Pilgrim 'Allegory.'" And Mircea Eliade, "Paradise and Utopia: Mythical Geography and Eschatology," in *Utopias and Utopian Thought*, ed. Frank E. Manuel (Boston: Houghton Mifflin, 1966), 260–80, at 276–77, comments on the image in the culture of a South American millenarian tribe. Its classic statement in American literature is by William Bradford, *Plymouth Plantation*, 1:124; and, of course, the Puritans of Plymouth have long been called the Pilgrim Fathers. Albert Matthews, "The Term *Pilgrim Fathers* and Early Celebrations of Forefathers' Day," *Publications of the Colonial Society of Massachusetts* 17 (1915): 300–392, esp. 352ff.

40. Diana Poulton, *John Dowland: His Life and Works* (Berkeley and Los Angeles: University of California Press, 1972), 299.

41. If Johnson used stanzas 1, 2, and 11 (the stanzas printed by Dowland), I would be certain of Johnson's intention.

42. Morton, *New English Canaan*, 279–80.

43. George Lyman Kittredge, "A Harvard Salutatory Oration of 1662," *Publications of the Colonial Society of Massachusetts* 28 (1930–33): 1–24. Samuel Eliot Morison, "The Reverend Seaborn Cotton's Commonplace Book," *Publications of the Colonial Society of Massachusetts* 32 (1933–37), 320–52. Phillips Barry, *Bulletin of the Folk Song Society of the North-East*, nos. 1–12 (1930–37; reprint, Philadelphia: American Folklore Society, Bibliographical and Special Series [vol. 11], 1960); and Carleton Sprague Smith, "Broadsides and Their Music in Colonial America," 157–64.

44. See my review of *The Diary of Michael Wigglesworth, 1653–1657*, ed. Edmund S. Morgan, in *Seventeenth-Century News* 24, iv (1966): item 13.

Appendixes

1. I give my reasons for adopting this title on p. 93.

2. Leonard W. Labaree, William B. Willcox et al., eds., *The Papers of Benjamin Franklin*, 22 vols. to 1982 (New Haven: Yale University Press, 1959–   ), 7:326–50.

3. A full description of Mecom's pamphlet is given below in part 1 of the Bibliography, "Chronological Checklist of 'New England's Annoyances' through 1916."

4. Griswold, Duyckinck, and all other brief references to reprintings of "New England's Annoyances" are fully identified in part 1 of the Bibliography, "Chronological Checklist" and briefly in part 2, "Repeated References."

5. I hypothesize that "New England's Annoyances" appeared as a broadside ballad, printed by Stephen Day at the Cambridge, Massachusetts, press in 1643. (My reasons for the date appear above in chapter 2.) Although no broadside poems from these years are extant, bibliographers have long attributed some elegies printed in Nathaniel Morton's *New Englands Memoriall* (Cambridge, 1669) to Day's press. Worthington Chauncey Ford, *Braodsides, Ballads &c. Printed in Massachusetts, 1639–1800* (Boston: Massachusetts Historical Society [vol. 75 of its *Collections*], 1922), nos. 6, 7, 9, 10, 25, 26, 32, and 34. See also George Parker Winship, *The Cambridge Press 1638–1692* (Philadelphia: University of Pennsylvania Press, 1945), 81–89.

6. Bartering was discussed above in chapter 2. Massachusetts did not issue its own paper currency until 1690. Eric P. Newman, *Bicentennial Edition of the Early Paper Money of America* (Racine, Wis.: Western Publishing, 1976), 142ff.

7. Edmund S. Morgan, in *Visible Saints: The History of a Puritan Idea*, 113–52, follows the decline in the late seventeenth century. Robert G. Pope, in both *The Half-Way Covenant: Church Membership in Puritan New England* (Princeton: Princeton University Press, 1969), esp. 272–73, and "New England Verses the New England Mind: The Myth of Declension," *Journal of Social History* 3 (1969): 95–108, argues against the idea of an increasingly secular society.

8. Colonial references to the tune "A Cobler There Was" appear in the *New York Gazette*, 20 May 1751, and the *South Carolina Gazette*, 20 November 1752. "Derry Down" was cited as the tune of an American song in the *London Magazine* 13 (August 1744): 406–7; and in the *South Carolina Gazette*, 3 July 1755. For the tune in the Revolutionary American newspapers, see Gillian B. Anderson, *Freedom's Voice in Poetry and Song* (Wilmington, Del.: Scholarly Resources, 1977), 473, 479, 498–81. "A Cobler There Was" is also the tune given in a broadside ballad entitled *A New Ballad, Upon a New Occasion* ([Philadelphia, 1771]), Evans 42255. Carleton Sprague Smith, "Broadsides and their Music in Colonial America," 292–95, discusses and reprints a Tory song of 1776 to the tune "King John and the Abbot of Canterbury" (another name for the "Derry Down" tune).

9. For versions of the tune and discussions, see Bertrand H. Bronson, *The Traditional Tunes of the Child Ballads*, 1:354–61; and Claude M. Simpson, *The British Broadside Ballad and its Music*, 172–76.

10. William Shaw Russell, "Airs of the Pilgrims," appended to his *Guide to Plymouth, and Recollections of the Pilgrims* (Boston: G. Coolidge, 1846), Appendix, 1n.

11. Evert Augustus Duyckinck and George L. Duyckinck, eds., *Cyclopaedia of American Literature*, 2 vols. (New York: C. Scribner, 1855), 1:68; *American Historical Record* 3 (1874): 53; William Peterfield Trent et al., eds., *The Cambridge History of American Literature*, 4 vols. (New York: Putnam's, 1917), 1:460; and Harold S. Jantz, "The First Century of New England Verse," *Proceedings of the American Antiquarian Society* 53 (1943): 502–3, all give the *Massachusetts Magazine* as the first printing.

12. "J. F." may have been James Freeman (1759–1835), Unitarian minister of King's Chapel, Boston, 1787–1826, and an editor of *The Boston Magazine* in 1783 and 1784. See Lyon N. Richardson, *A History of Early American Magazines 1741–1789* (New York: Thomas Nelson and Sons, 1931), 213, 217–19, 222.

13. Johnson even changed the original word "do" to "doth" in l. 15 of *The Passion of a Discontented Mind* when he borrowed its first four stanzas. See n. 36 in chapter 4, above.

14. In 1971, through the courtesy of Mr. L. D. Geller, Director of Pilgrim Hall, Plymouth, Massachusetts, I examined the papers of Deacon Ephraim Spooner (1735–1818) but found neither a manuscript of "New England's Annoyances" nor any correspondence from Dr. Benjamin Waterhouse.

15. "Biographical Sketches of the Life and Character of the late Gov. Bowden" appeared on pp. 5–8 of the January 1791 *Massachusetts Magazine*. "Our Forefathers' Song" is on p. 52.

16. For Harold Jantz's reconstruction, see Harrison T. Meserole, ed., *Seventeenth-Century American Poetry* (New York: New York University Press, 1968), 503–5.

17. Lewis was elected to membership on 24 August 1830 and resigned on 25 January 1844. *Proceedings of the Massachusetts Historical Society* 1 (1791–1835): 434; and 2 (1835–55): 264.

18. On the typical changes made in the process of oral transmission, see Phillips Barry, "The Transmission of Folk Song," *Journal of American Folk-Lore* 27 (1914): 67–76; "The Nature of Ballad Variation," in *The Ballad of Tradition*, Gordon Hall Gerould (Oxford: At the University Press, 1932); W. Edson Richmond, "Some Effects of Verbal and Typographical

Error on Oral Transmission," *Southern Folklore Quarterly* 15 (1951): 159–70; Douglas J. McMillan, "A Survey of Theories Concerning the Oral Transmission of the Traditional Ballad," *Southern Folklore Quarterly* 28 (1964): 299–309; and the statements and references in Alan Dundes, ed., *The Study of Folklore* (Englewood Cliffs, N.J.: Prentice-Hall, 1965), 243–47.

19. So my friend the late Professor Claude Simpson (1910–76) assured me on 1 October 1974.

20. See above, n. 10.

21. Robert R. Walcott, "Husbandry in Colonial New England," *New England Quarterly* 9 (1936): 228, 240, and 248. At a Woburn, Massachussetts town meeting, 14 February 1652/3, "It was ordered . . . that all fences shall be as sufficient as a good four rail fence, where any corn is planted, and that all swine shall be yoked and rung, according to a former order; provided that after any swine have taken a taste of any corn by breaking into any man's corn, after complaint, such swine shall be kept up for after time." Edward Johnson, "Woburn Records, 1640–1672," ed. Edward F. Johnson and William R. Cutter, *Woburn Journal*, 1888, p. 13, the Harvard University Library, shelf-number US 13530. 3f*. See also Bridenbaugh, *Fat Mutton*, 40–41.

22. Samuel Eliot Morison, *The Story of the "Old Colony" of New Plymouth* (New York: A. A. Knopf, 1956), 98n.

23. Joseph Albert Ernst surveys the background in *Money and Politics in America 1755–1775* (Chapel Hill: University of North Carolina Press, 1973). See also Curtis Nettels, *Money Supply of the American Colonies before 1720* (Madison: University of Wisconsin Press, 1934).

Bibliographies

Chronological Checklist of "New England's Annoyances" through 1916

1758

A Text. "*An Old Song, wrote by one of our first* New-England *Planters, on their Management in those* good *Old Times. To the Tune* of A Cobler there was, etc.*" In *Father Abraham's Speech to a great Number of People, at a Vendue of Merchant-Goods; Introduced to the Publick by Poor Richard . . . To which are added, Seven curious Pieces of Writing.* Boston: Benjamin Mecom. [1758], p. 23. Collation: [1–2], 3–22, [23–24], pp. 12 mo., [A]⁴, B², C⁴, D².

The title is taken from the contents, p. 2, and the text of "An old Song" is found on p. 23, the penultimate page of the pamphlet.

Wilberforce Eames, "The Antigua Press and Benjamin Mecom, 1748–1765," *Proceedings of the American Antiquarian Society*, n.s., 38 (1928): 303–48, lists this pamphlet (which contains the first separate printing of Franklin's *Way to Wealth* under its earlier title) as no. 9 on 326–27 and notes, "It was advertised as 'This Day Published,' in the *Boston News Letter*, No. 2907, for Thursday, March 30, 1758; repeated on April 7 and 13. Also in the *Boston Gazette, and Country Journal*, No. 157 for Monday, April 3, 1758; repeated on April 10 and 17." It was also advertised in the *New Hampshire Gazette*, 8 September 1758. Although no copy was known to be extant when Eames compiled his bibliography in 1928, several copies have since turned up. The Massachusetts Historical Society copy has twice been reprinted in facsimile: as Massachusetts Historical Society, *Photostat Americana*, 2d ser., no. 104 (Boston, 1940); and as a Christmas souvenir for G. K. Hall & Co., ([Boston], 1963). The John Carter Brown Library copy has been reprinted in facsimile in *The Complete Poor Richard Almanacs*, intro. by Whitfield J. Bell, Jr., 2 vols. (Barre, Mass.: Imprint Society, 1970), 2 : 397–420.

None of the eighteenth-century reprintings of *Father Abraham's Speech* include the "Old Song." See Shipton-Mooney, p. 281A, where the following reprints are listed: Boston: Mecom, [1760], E41122; New London: Green, [1760], E41123; New Haven: [1764], "A ghost of 10619," E9665; and New Haven, [1767], E10619.

The 1807 reprinting (see below) of *Father Abraham's Speech* does include the "Old Song."

References: Evans 8131 (which locates copies at Boston Public Library and New York Public Library) is really describing Mecom's 1760 reprinting, but the American Antiquarian Society microcard reprints the original 1758 printing); Sabin 70909 (no. B, mistakenly dated 1760); Shipton-Mooney, pp. 262A and 281A; and NF 0339539 (mistaken in pagination and in collation), locating copies at Yale, the Massachusetts Historical Society, the John Carter Brown Library, and the American Antiquarian Society.

1774

B Text. "an old ballad composed and sung by some of the first settlers of New-England, called New-England's annoyances, recollected and repeated lately, by an old lady of 92 years of age." In *The Massachusetts Spy*, 3 February 1774, p. 4, col. 1.

Reprinted in the *Nova Scotia Gazette*, 5 April 1774, p. 4, cols. 2–3, and in Albert Matthews, "Old Ballad called New-England's Annoyances," *Publications of the Colonial Society of Massachusetts* 18 (1915–16): 158–59.

1791

C Text. "Our Forefather's Song. Composed about the year 1630." In *The Massachusetts Magazine* 3 (January 1791): 52–53. An endnote adds that *"The above, was taken memoriter, from the lips of an old Lady, at the advanced period of* 92."

1807

"An Old Song—Tune—A Cobler there was." In *Father Abraham's Speech . . . to which are added Several Curious Pieces of Writing*. Dedham, N.H.: H. Mann for William Tileston Clapp, 1807, pp. 22–23.

A reprint of *A* Text, 1758. Although the stanzas are not numbered and although the common nouns are generally not capitalized, there are no substantive differences from *A* Text.

References: Sabin 25508. Shaw and Shoemaker, 12591. NF 0339614, locating copies at the Library of Congress and Harvard.

1822

D Text. "The hardships and fare of the first planters of New England. An old song One Hundred and fifty years ago." In *Old Colony Memorial*, 18 May 1822, p. 1, col. 4—p. 2, col. 1. An accompanying letter from Dr. Benjamin Waterhouse to Deacon Ephraim Spooner identifies the source of the song as an "old lady . . . who repeated these verses in 1767, when 94 years of age."

1824

E Text. "Forefather's Song. [Composed about the year 1630, taken *memoriter* in 1791, from the lips of an old lady, at the advanced age of 92]." In John Farmer and Jacob Bailey Moore, eds., *Collections Historical and Miscellaneous: and Monthly Literary Journal* 3 (1824): 230–31.

1829

F Text. "The following song, which appears to have been written about this time [1630], exhibits some of the peculiar customs and modes of thinking among the early settlers." In Alonzo Lewis, *The History of Lynn*, [*Massachusetts*]. Boston: J. H. Eastburn, 1829, p. 35.

Reprinted in the later editions of Lewis, *History of Lynn*, 1844, 1865, and 1890. Also reprinted in John Warner Barber, *Historical Collections . . . of . . . Massachusetts*. Worcester, Mass.: Dorr, Howland, and Co., 1839.

1838

G Text. "OUR FOREFATHER'S SONG. [Composed about the year 1630, author unknown, *taken memoriter, in 1785, from the lips of an old Lady, at the advanced period of 96 . . .*]" In *Collections of the Massachusetts Historical Society*, 3d ser., 7 (1838): 29–30.

1839

"The following song. . . ." In John Warner Barber, ed., *Historical Collections . . . of . . . Massachusetts*. Worcester, Mass.: Dorr, Howland, and Co., 1839, p. 195.

Reprinted from Alonzo Lewis, *History of Lynn*, 1829.

Reprinted in the later editions of Barber, 1840, 1841, 1844, and 1846.

1842

Untitled. In Rufus Wilmot Griswold, ed., *The Poets and Poetry of America*. Philadelphia: Carey and Hart, 1842, p. xiii.

Reprinted in the numerous later editions of Griswold's anthology.

1846

"Our Forefathers' Song. The Hardships and Fare of the First Planters in New England. Repeated by an old lady, aged 94 years, in 1767." In William Shaw Russell, *Guide to Plymouth, and Recollections of the Pilgrims*. Appendix, "Airs of the Pilgrims." Boston: Privately printed, 1846, pp. 1–3.

Russell, p. 3, quotes a letter from Benjamin Waterhouse to Ephraim Spooner, dated Cambridge, 15 December 1817, which enclosed a copy of the poem. Although Russell had seen both *D* text (1822) and *G* text (1838), he made "a very few verbal alterations" in this text in order "to adapt it to music" (p. 3). In a footnote on p. 1, Russell said "these popular lines would find appropriate music in the old tune of *Derry Down*."

"A Song of Olden Time." In *American Penny Magazine* 2 (17 October 1846): 592.

This text in "oulde" style spelling credits the *New Haven Courier* as its source.

1853

"Our Forefathers' Song." In William Henry Bartlett, *The Pilgrim Fathers: or, The Founders of New England in the Reign of James the First*. London: Arthur Hall, Virtue and Co., 1853, p. 20.

Bartlett reprints twenty lines from Russell, *Guide to Plymouth*, 1846.

1855

"Our Forefathers' Song." In Evert Augustus Duyckinck and George L. Duyckinck, eds., *Cyclopaedia of American Literature*, 2 vols. New York: C. Scribner, 1855, 1:68.

Duyckinck refers to both the *Massachusetts Magazine* (1791) text and to the *Massachusetts Historical Society Collections* (1838) text.

Reprinted in the second edition (1875) of Duyckinck's *Cyclopaedia*, 1:73.

1858

"New England's Annoyances." In William Evans Burton, *Cyclopaedia of Wit and Humor*, 2 vols. New York: Appleton, 1858, 1:2–3. Evidently reprinted from Griswold (1842).

1865

"New England's Annoyances." In John W. S. Hows, ed. *Golden Leaves from the American Poets*. New York: J. J. Gregory, 1865, pp. 1–2. Evidently reprinted from Burton (1858).

1872

"New England's Annoyances." In William Michael Rossetti, *American Poems*. London: E. Moxson, 1872, pp. 1–2. Evidently reprinted from Hows (1865).

1874

"Our Forefathers' Song." *American Historical Record* 3 (1874): 53.

John William Potts sent in this text from the *Massachusetts Magazine*, 1791.

1878

"New England's Annoyances." In W. J. Linton, ed., *Poetry of America*. London: G. Bell and Sons, 1878, pp. xxiv-xxv. Evidently reprinted from Hows (1865).

1891

"New England's Annoyances." In James Barr, ed., *American Humorous Verse*. London: Walter Scott, [1891], pp. 1–3.

1903

Untitled. In Edward Everett Hale, ed. *New England History in Ballads*. Boston: Little, Brown and Co., 1903, pp. 16–18.

Mysteriously, Hale says that the lines "were first printed in 1773, having been preserved traditionally." His text, however, seems to follow *G* text (1838), although he has been influenced by *F* text (1829) and has supplied several of his own "improvements."

1907

"New England's Annoyances." *The Magazine of History* 5 (March 1907): 153–54. Evidently reprinted from Griswold (1842).

1908

"New England's Annoyances." In Burton Egbert Stevenson, ed., *Poems of*

American History. Boston: Houghton Mifflin, 1908, pp. 65–66. Cites Griswold, 1854 (1st ed., 1842) and the *Massachusetts Historical Society Collections*, 1838.

Reprinted in the later editions of Stevenson, 1922, 1936, and 1950.

1916

"Our Forefathers' Song." In Albert Matthews, "Old Ballad Called New England's Annoyances," *Publications of the Colonial Society of Massachusetts* 18 (1915–16): 156–59.

Matthews refers to the *Massachusetts Magazine* (1791) text, the *Massachusetts Historical Society Collections* (1838) text, and reprints the *Massachusetts Spy* (1774) text. In 1914, the earliest text Matthews knew was the *Massachusetts Magazine* (1791); see *Publications of the Colonial Society of Massachusetts* 17 (1913–14): 302 n.

Repeated References

This bibliography lists all repeated references. It does not include works to which only one reference is made, and it does not include all of those works listed in the "Chronological Checklist of 'New England's Annoyances.'"

Albertson. Dean. "Puritan Liquor in the Planting of New England." *New England Quarterly* 23 (1950): 477–90.

Arber, Edward, and A. G. Bradley, eds. *Travels and Works of Captain John Smith*. 2 vols. Edinburgh: John Grant, 1910.

Barbour, Philip L., ed. *The Jamestown Voyages Under the First Charter 1606–1609*. 2 vols. Cambridge: Hakluyt Society, 1969.

Bradford, William. *The Collected Verses*. Edited by Michael G. Runyon. St. Paul, Minn.: John Colet Press, 1974.

———. *History of Plymouth Plantation 1620–1647*. Edited by Worthington Chauncey Ford. 2 vols. Boston: Houghton Mifflin, 1912.

Bridenbaugh, Carl. *Fat Mutton and Liberty of Conscience: Society in Rhode Island, 1636–1690*. Providence: Brown University Press, 1974.

Bronson, Bertrand Harris. *The Traditional Tunes of the Child Ballads*. 4 vols. Princeton: Princeton University Press, 1959–72.

Brooks, Harold Fletcher. "Rump Songs; an Index with Notes." *Publication of the Oxford Bibliographical Society* 5 (1940).

Bullough, Geoffrey. "The Later History of Cockaigne." In *Festschrift Prof. Dr. Herbert Koziolzum Siebzigsten Geburtstag*, edited by Gero Bauer, Franz K. Stanzel, and Franz Zaic. Stuttgart: Wilhelm Baraunmuller [*Wiener Beitrage zur englischen Philologie* 75], 1973, pp. 22–35.

Burton, William Evans. *Cyclopaedia of Wit and Humor.* 2 vols. New York: Appleton, 1858.

Carroll, Peter N. *Puritanism and the Wilderness: The Intellectual Significance of the New England Frontier, 1629–1700.* New York: Columbia University Press, 1969.

Case, Arthur E. *A Bibliography of English Poetical Miscellanies 1521–1750.* Oxford: Bibliographical Society, 1935.

Crum, Margaret. *The First-Line Index of English Poetry, 1500–1800 in Manuscripts of the Bodleian Library.* 2 vols. Oxford: Clarendon Press, 1969.

Day, Cyrus Lawrence, and Eleanor Boswell Murrie. *English Song Books 1561–1702.* London: Bibliographical Society, 1940.

Dexter, Henry Martin, ed. *Mourt's Relation or Journal of the Plantation at Plymouth.* Boston: J. K. Wiggin, 1865.

A Dictionary of Americanisms on Historical Principles. Edited by Mitford M. Mathews. 2 vols. Chicago: University of Chicago Press, 1951.

A Dictionary of American English on Historical Principles. Edited by William A. Craigie et al. 4 vols. Chicago: University of Chicago Press, 1936–44.

The Dictionary of National Biography. Edited by Leslie Stephen and Sidney Lee. 66 vols. [London:] Oxford University Press, 1885–1900.

Dudley, Thomas. "Letter to the Countess of Lincoln, March, 1631." In *Letters from New England.* Edited by Everett Emerson. Amherst: University of Massachusetts Press, 1976, pp. 67–83.

[Dunster, Henry and Thomas Weld.] *New Englands First Fruits* (1643). In *The Founding of Harvard College.* Edited by Samuel Eliot Morison. Cambridge: Harvard University Press, 1935, pp. 420–47.

D'Urfey, Thomas. *Wit and Mirth: or Pills to Purge Melancholy.* 6 vols. London: W. Pearson for J. Tonson, 1719.

Earle, Alice Morse. *Customs and Fashions in Old New England.* New York: Charles Scribner's Sons, 1893.

Ebsworth, Joseph Woodfall, ed. *Choyce Drollery.* Boston; Lincolnshire: R. Roberts, 1876.

———, ed. *Merry Drollery Compleat.* Boston: Lincolnshire: R. Roberts, 1875.

Ebsworth, Joseph Woodfall, and William Chappell, eds. *Roxburghe Ballads.* 8 vols. London: The Ballad Society, 1869–99. Reprint. New York: AMS Press, 1967.

Eliot, John. "Letter to Sir Simonds D'Ewes" (1633). In *Letters from New England: The Massachusetts Bay Colony 1629–1638,* edited by Everett Emerson, 104–8. Amherst: University of Massachusetts Press, 1976, pp. 104–8.

Emerson, Everett, ed. *Letters from New England: The Massachusetts Bay Colony 1629–1638.* Amherst: University of Massachusetts Press, 1976.

Firth, Charles H., ed. *An American Garland: Being a Collection of Ballads Relating to America 1563–1759.* Oxford: Blackwell, 1915.

———. "[The ballad history of] The Reign of Charles I." *Transactions of the Royal Historical Society,* 3d ser., 6 (1912): 19–64.

Franklin, Benjamin. *The Papers of Benjamin Franklin.* Edited by Leonard W. Labaree and William B. Willcox et al. 22 vols. to 1982. New Haven: Yale University Press, 1959–.

———. *The Writings of Benjamin Franklin.* Edited by Albert H. Smyth. 10 vols. New York: Macmillan Co., 1905–7.

Gallagher, Edward. "The Case of the *Wonder-Working Providence.*" *Bulletin of the New York Public Library* 77 (1973): 10–27.

———. "An Overview of Edward Johnson's *Wonder-Working Providence.*" *Early American Literature* 5 (1971): 30–49.

———. "The *Wonder-Working* Providence as Spiritual Biography. *Early American Literature* 10 (1975): 75–87.

Griswold, Rufus Wilmot. *The Poets and Poetry of America.* Philadelphia: Carey and Hart, 1842.

Haller, William. *The Rise of Puritanism.* New York: Columbia University Press, 1938.

Hardeman, Nicholas P. *Shucks, Shocks, and Hominy Blocks: Corn as a Way of Life in Pioneer America.* Baton Rouge: Louisiana University Press, 1981.

Harris, Thaddeus M. *Memorials of the First Church in Dorchester.* Boston: Daily Advertiser, 1830.

Higginson, Francis. "Letters to His Friends in England" (1629). In *Letters from New England: The Massachusetts Bay Colony 1629–1638,* edited by Everett Emerson. Amherst: University of Massachusetts Press, 1976, pp. 12–27.

———. *New England's Plantation* (1630). In *Letters from New England: The Massachusetts Bay Colony 1629–1638,* edited by Everett Emerson. Amherst: University of Massachusetts Press, 1976, pp. 29–38.

Hooker, Thomas. *Survey of the Summe of Church Discipline.* London: A. M. for John Bellamy, 1648. Reprint. New York: Arno Press, 1972.

Hows, John W. S., ed. *Golden Leaves from the American Poets.* New York: J. J. Gregory, 1856.

Hutchinson, Thomas. *The History of the Colony and Province of Massachusetts-Bay.* Edited by Lawrence Shaw Mayo. 3 vols. Cambridge: Harvard University Press, 1936.

Jantz, Harold S. "American Baroque: Three Representative Poets." In *Discoveries and Considerations: Essays on Early American Literature and Aes-*

thetics Presented to Harold Jantz, edited by Calvin Israel, 3–23. Albany: State University of New York Press, 1976.

————. *The First Century of New England Verse*. 1943. Reprint. New York: Russell and Russell, 1962.

[Johnson, Edward.] *Good News from New England*. London: M. Simmons, 1648.

————. *History of New England* (London, 1654). Edited by J. Franklin Jameson. New York: Scribners, 1910.

————. "Woburn Town Records." In *Woburn Journal* (1888). Copy at Harvard University, shelf number US 13530. 3F*.

[Larsen, Esther Louise.] "Peter Kalm's Description of Maize." *Agricultural History* 9 (1935): 98–117.

Lechford, Thomas. *Plain Dealing or News from New England* (1642). Edited by J. Hammond Trumbull. Boston: Wiggin & Lunt, 1867.

Lemay, J. A. Leo. "Benjamin Franklin." In *Major Writers of Early American Literature*, edited by Everett Emerson, 205–43. Madison: University of Wisconsin Press, 1972.

————. "The Frontiersman From Lout to Hero." *Proceedings of the American Antiquarian Society* 88 (1979): 187–224.

————. *Men of Letters in Colonial Maryland*. Knoxville: University of Tennessee Press, 1972.

————. "The Tall Tales of a Colonial Frontiersman." *Western Pennsylvania Historical Magazine* 64 (1981): 33–46.

————. "The Text, Tradition, and Themes of 'The Big Bear of Arkansas.'" *American Literature* 47 (1975–76): 321–42.

Levermore, Charles H. *Forerunners and Competitors of the Pilgrims and Puritans 1601–1625*. 2 vols. Brooklyn, N.Y.: New England Society of Brooklyn, 1912.

Levett, Christopher. *A Voyage into New England*. London: W. Jones, 1628. Reprint. *Collections of the Massachusetts Historical Society* 3d ser., 8 (1843): 159–90.

Loyal Songs. London, 1731. Case, no. 128 ld.

Massachusetts Records. Edited by Nathaniel B. Shurtleff. In *Records of the Governor and Company of the Massachusetts Bay in New England*. Boston: William White, 1853.

Matthews, Albert. "Old Ballad Called New England's Annoyances." *Publications of the Colonial Society of Massachusetts* 18 (1915–16): 156–59

Merry Drollery. London: Printed by J. W. for P. H., [1661]. Case, no. 132 la.

Merry Drollery. London: Printed for Simon Miller, 1670. Case, no. 132 (b).

Merry Drollery Complete. London: Printed for Simon Miller, 1670. Case, no. 132 (b).

Mood, Filmer. "John Winthrop, Jr. on Indian Corne." *New England Quarterly* 10 (1937): 121–33.

Morgan, Edmund S. *Visible Saints: The History of a Puritan Idea.* New York: New York University Press, 1963. Reprint. Ithaca: Cornell University Press, 1965.

Morison, Samuel Eliot. *Builders of the Bay Colony.* Boston: Houghton Mifflin, 1930.

———. *The Founding of Harvard College.* Cambridge: Harvard University Press, 1935.

Morton, Thomas. *New English Canaan* (1637). Edited by Charles Francis Adams. Boston: Prince Society, 1883.

The Oxford English Dictionary. Edited by James A. H. Murray et al. 13 vols. 1884–1928. Reprint. Oxford: University Press, 1933.

A Supplement to the Oxford English Dictionary. 2 vols. Oxford: Clarendon Press, 1972 and 1976.

Poole, William Frederick, ed. *The Wonder-Working Providence of Sions Saviour in New England. By Edward Johnson.* Andover, Mass.: Warren F. Draper, 1867.

Rimbault, Edward F. *A Little Book of Songs and Ballads.* London: J. R. Smith, 1851.

Rollins, Hyder E. *An Analytical Index to the Ballad Entries (1557–1709) in the Registers of the Company of Stationers of London.* Chapel Hill: University of North Carolina Press, 1924. Reprint. Hatboro, Pa.: Tradition Press, 1967.

Rump. 2 vols. London: Printed for Henry Brome at the Gun and Henry Marsh at the Princes Armes, 1662. Case, no. 128(b).

Russel, William Shaw. *Guide to Plymouth, and Recollections of the Pilgrims.* Boston: G. Cooledge, 1846.

Rutman, Darrett B. "Governor Winthrop's Garden Crop: The Significance of Agriculture in the Early Commerce of Massachusetts Bay." *William and Mary Quarterly,* 3d ser., 20 (1963): 396–415.

Sabin, Joseph. *Biblioteca Americana.* 29 vols. New York: Bibliographical Society of America, 1868–1936.

Scholes, Percy A. *The Puritans and Music in England and New England.* London: Oxford University Press, 1934.

Scull, G. D. "English Ballads about New England." *New England Historic and Genealogic Register* 36 (1882): 359–62.

The Second Part of Merry Drollery. London: Printed by J. W. for P.H. [1661.] Case, no. 132 (2)(a).

Simpson, Claude M. *The British Broadside Ballad and Its Music.* New Brunswick: Rutgers University Press, 1966.

Smith, Carleton Sprague. "Broadsides and Their Music in Colonial America." In *Music in Colonial Massachusetts 1630–1820. I: Music in Public Places.* Boston: Colonial Society of Massachusetts, *Collections* 53 (1980): 157–367.

Smith, John. *Travels and Works of Captain John Smith.* Edited by Edward Arber and A. G. Bradley. 2 vols. Edinburgh: John Grant, 1910.

Stearns, Raymond P. *Science in the British Colonies of America.* Urbana: University of Illinois Press, 1970.

Tichi, Cecelia. *New World, New Earth: Environmental Reform in American Literature from the Puritans through Whitman.* New Haven: Yale University Press, 1979.

Tompson, Benjamin. *Benjamin Tompson: Colonial Bard.* Edited by Peter White. College Park: Pennsylvania State University Press, 1980.

Walcott, Robert R. "Husbandry in Colonial New England." *New England Quarterly* 9 (1936): 218–52.

Ward, Nathaniel. *The Simple Cobler of Aggawam in America* (1647). Edited by P. M. Zall. Lincoln: University of Nebraska Press, 1969.

[White, John.] *The Planters Plea. On the Grounds of Plantations Examined and usuall objections Answered.* London: W. Iones, 1630. Reprinted in "Founding of Massachusetts." *Proceedings of the Massaschusetts Historical Society* 62 (1930): 367–427.

Williams, Roger. *A Key into the Language of America* (1643). Edited by John J. Teunissen and Evelyn J. Hinz. Detroit: Wayne State University Press, 1973.

Wing, Donald. *Short-Title Catalogue.* 3 vols. New York: Modern Language Association, 1972.

Winslow, Edward. *Good News from New England* (1624). In *Chronicles of the Pilgrim Fathers*, edited by Alexander Young, 269–374. Boston: Little and Brown, 1841.

Winthrop, John. *Journal.* Printed as *The History of New England 1630–1649.* Edited by James Savage. 2 vols. 2d ed. Boston: Little, Brown, 1853.

Winthrop Papers. Edited by Allyn Bailey Forbes et al. 5 vols. [Boston:] Massachusetts Historical Society, 1929–47.

Wit and Drollery. London, 1661. Case, no. 114(b).

Wood, William. *New England's Prospect* (1634). Edited by Alden T. Vaughan. Amherst: University of Massachusetts Press, 1977.

Young, Alexander, ed. *Chronicles of the Pilgrim Fathers.* Boston: Little, Brown, 1841.

Index

Note: NEA is used throughout for "New England's Annoyances."